GW00645402

£7.50

THE HERALD OF COMING GOOD

Contrary to the established custom, I shall not only permit this first book of mine, as well as the books of the first series, to be reprinted in any country, but, if necessary, I am willing to subsidize it, on the condition of course that absolute accuracy is preserved.

G. GURDJIEFF.

THE HERALD OF COMING GOOD

COMING GOOD

G.I. Gurdjieff

**Sure Fire
Press**

ISBN # 0-916411-72-9

*** 1988 ***
PRINTED IN THE U.S.A. BY
SURE FIRE PRESS
P.O. BOX 623
EDMONDS, WA 98020

G. GURDJIEFF

THE HERALD OF COMING GOOD

FIRST APPEAL
TO CONTEMPORARY HUMANITY

Price from 8 to 108
French francs

Consult next page **

PARIS
1933

⁎⁎⁎ Inspired as I am by a deep conviction, springing from a long line of experimental elucidations and deductions pointing to the conclusion that, if a man desire sincerely and seriously, and out of no mere curiosity, to attain to the knowledge of the way leading to Real Being, and if he fulfil to this end all that is requested of him and begin, in fact, among other things to aid indirectly, and from his very first step, the attainment of this by others, he will, by this act alone, become as it were the forming ground for the real data contributing to the manifestation of objective and actual Good ; and animated as I am by the general intention of arriving finally, by means of my literary arguments and public demonstrations proposed for the near future of experimental elucidations, at the instilling into the consciousness of my contemporaries of several such ,, psychic-initiative " factors as in my opinion as well as in that of every man capable of a little impartial meditation ought inevitably to act as guiding principles in the consciousness of all creatures presuming to call themselves " God-Like ", of such " initiative " factors, namely, as should certainly include the factor inducing men both to react instinctively and, upon reflection, to realize clearly the moral obligation to help one's neighbour,—I have now decided upon the very act of selling and of spreading far and wide the contents of this first of my writings intended to head the list of my publications and directed, by the fulfilment of the task- originally imposed upon myself, to initiate of itself in man's consciousness the formation of the aforesaid and, for the communal life of people, important " psychic " factor.

Accordingly, as I have the intention, on the one hand, of affording to a multitude of Our Common Father's creatures, who bear your likeness, but whose means are for some reason or other limited, the possibility of acquiring this first booklet of mine free of charge, and as I have, on the other hand, certain definite plans bearing upon the next publication of my writings, I have deliberately decided not to fix any definite price for this booklet, leaving it to the free will of the purchaser to pay from 8 to 108 French francs.

I shall at the same time, and without entering into the usual contemporary discussions about life, expressly request all those who happen to acquire this first booklet of mine to answer three questions, which will be set them by the seller so as to permit him to fill in the corresponding paragraphs of the " Registration-Blank " herewith appended.

The AUTHOR.

REGISTRATION - BLANK

appended to

THE HERALD OF COMING GOOD

N⁰ 00979

1. *Name of purchaser* ....

....

....

2. *Address* ....

....

3. *Acquired accidentaly or on advice* ....

....

....

4. *Who advised? Give name and address* ....

....

....

5. *Sum paid* ....

....

Signature of seller

MY FIRST PRACTICAL COUNSEL.

I counsel all readers, who have at any time met me upon the ground of my ideas, to postpone reading this first appeal until they have, concentrating in their nature as well as in their thoughts and feelings, grasped the essence of the content of the circular letter appended to the booklet, and have at the same time previously acquainted themselves with the " Registration-Blank " attached to this latter and which will be of practical import for acquiring the books of my first series of writings.

G. GURDJIEFF.

A highly original and, to me, even troublingly strange
coincidence of several very defined and entirely different
factors, arising out of my activity and having bearing
upon today, not only compels, but also inspires me to
mark this day by a refusal to bide a more convenient time
and by an intention to begin on this very day an exposition
of the first of the seven appeals which, among others,
I decided to address during my period of activity as a
writer to the whole of contemporary humanity.

I shall begin by explaining the particular nature of
this strange coincidence.

First of all, expounding as I have done night and day
for almost ten years all kinds of fragments of the general
mass of information intended by me for publication, I
have, as it happens, finished only this day a preliminary
compilation of the material designed for this purpose.

Secondly, engaged as I have been in the course of the
last three years in the completion, parallel to this, of the
first series of writings intended to head the list of my
publications, I have also finally completed this work on
precisely this day.

Thirdly and finally,—today is the last day of the term I
had assigned to myself twenty one years ago,—of the
term during which I had, according to the special oath

11

I took, bound myself in my conscience to lead in some ways an artificial life, modelled upon a programme which had been previously planned in accordance with certain definite principles.

Before venturing to unfold the very substance of my first appeal to contemporary humanity, I count it essential and even in every way my duty, to set forth—even if only approximately—the motives which compelled me to assume the whole burden of such an artificial life.

This protracted and, for me, absolutely unnatural life, absolutely irreconcilable, too, in every way with the traits that had entrenched themselves in my individuality by the time of my maturity, was the direct consequence of my decision, founded upon the results of my previous study of a whole series of historic precedents with a view, first of all,—to preventing, by to a certain degree unnatural outward manifestations of myself, the formation, in relation to me, of that already noted from ancient times " something ", termed by the great Solomon, King of Juda, " **Tzvarnoharno** ", which, as was set out by our ancestors, forms itself by a natural process in the communal life of people as an outcome of a conjunction of the evil actions of so-called " common people " and leads to the destruction of both him that tries to achieve something for general human welfare and of all that he has already accomplished to this end. Secondly, with a view,—to counteracting the manifestation in people with whom I came in contact of that inherent trait which, embedded as it is in the psyche of people and acting as an impediment to the realization of my aims, evokes from them, when confronted with other more or less prominent people, the functioning of the feeling of enslavement, paralysing once and for all their capacity for displaying the personal initiative of which I then stood in particular need.

My aim at that time was concentrated upon the creation of conditions permitting the comprehensive elucidation of one complicated and with difficulty explicable aspect of the question which had, already long before the beginning of this my artificial life, inhered in my being, and the necessity of whose final solution has, whether by the will of fate or thanks to the inscrutable laws of heredity, become and would, at the moment, appear to be the fundamental aim of my whole life and of the force motivating my activity.

I find myself obliged—in this, so to say, definitive statement as a writer, which will also have to serve among other things as a sort of " prospectus " of the new phase of my unremitting activity for the welfare of my neighbours,—to give a brief outline of the history of the rise and development of those events and causes which were responsible for the formation in my individuality of the unquenchable striving to solve this question, which had, in the end, become for me what modern psychologists might term an " irresistible Mania ".

This mania began to impose itself upon my being at the time of my youth when I was on the point of attaining responsible age and consisted in what I would now term an " irrepressible striving " to understand clearly the precise significance, in general, of the life process on earth of all the outward forms of breathing creatures and, in particular, of the aim of human life in the light of this interpretation.

Although a multitude of very specific factors, conditioned by my upbringing and education, had served as the primal cause for the formation in my being of the ground giving rise to such, for contemporary man, unusual striving, yet, as I understood later upon giving thought to the matter, the principal cause must in the end be attributed to those entirely accidental circumstances of my life which coincided precisely with the aforesaid transition from preparatory age to responsible age, and which may all be summed up in the fact that all my contacts at the time were almost exclusively with such persons of my age or my seniors who were either in the process of being formed themselves or who had already been formed into precisely that, of late increased amongst us, " psychic typicality " of people, the formation of which, as I myself have statistically established during the existence of my foundation, " **The Institute For Man's Harmonious Development** ", is due to the fact that the future representatives of this " typicality " have never, either with a view to the real understanding of actuality, or in the period of their preparatory age, or, again, in the period of their responsible life, absolutely never, and in spite of the obvious necessity of such a step, laid themselves open to experience, but have contented themselves with other people's fantasies, forming from them illusory conceptions and, at the same time, limiting themselves to intercourse with those like them, and have automatised themselves to a point of engaging upon authoritative discussions of all kinds of seemingly scientific, but, for the most part, abstract themes.

Although I, too, at that period of my life, resembled them in my outward manifestations, since I was as much a product as they were of the same abnormal conditions of environment, yet, thanks to the circumstance that I was in my nature, since childhood, already possessed, through the deliberate inculcation of both my father and my first tutor, of certain data permitting the development in my individuality, by the time of my responsible age, among several other very original and inherent traits, of this peculiar trait of inevitable impulse and striving to understand the very essence of any object that attracted my attention out of the ordinary, there began to form in my thoughts, gradually and even in a way imperceptibly to my waking consciousness, the " something ", which assumed definition soon after a strong spiritual tribulation caused by the death of an intimate friend, and this newly formed datum of my mind has begun ever since, upon contact with the so-called " cogitative-laura ", the product usually of the frequent repetition of certain defined and automatically current associations in man's mind, to engender in my entirety what I have elsewhere termed an " irrepressible striving ".

At first, the manifestation of this strange " psychic-factor " influenced only my mental activity, but did not derange me as a whole, that is, the effects of this manifestation did not hinder the established functioning of either my physical organism, with its psycho-nervous system, or the spirit, in the pure sense of the word, and I could, even in periods of pronounced resistance to the influence of this manifestation, by an effort of will or by an artificial stimulation of the mental and emotive associations proceeding within me, so control them as to prevent, so to speak, the " feeding " of this manifestation, and, in that way, to arrest the possibility of the continuation in my entirety of the formation of such undesirable impulses. A little later, upon the inception in my thoughts of this " something ", and as an obvious result of my meeting frequently and discussing this " idée fixe " of mine with numerous people, about whom I formed, in my as yet not " subjectivized " consciousness, and thanks to the widespread opinions of certain great authorities concerning these so-called " wiseacring " questions, certain precise impressions automatically influencing my general psyche, and as, in the course of diccussion with these authorities, as I represent it to myself now, there revived within me a sense of the full seriousness and profundity of these questions, the consequences and the real " significance " of the manifestations peculiar to this extraordinary striving gradually began to make themselves felt in all the parts whose totality coincided with my Being and, sometimes, even to influence their general functioning, that is, in a word, to penetrate into the " marrow-of-my-bones ".

The degree of fusion with my Being and the dominating influence on my psyche of this peculiar factor were such, that, after four or five years, I fell completely under its power, and since then it has, like an " itching-itch ", constantly compelled the whole of me or the separate parts of my general individuality, cost what it may, to elucidate everything for the cognition of all which can serve for the final solution of these, for me, cardinal questions.

Having become in my inner life, in the full sense of the word, a slave of such " aim ", obviously instilled by the Will of Fate in my entirety, from that time onwards, first compelled only by it, and shortly afterwards also stimulated quite often by my own consciousness, I lived absorbed in these researches until the year 1892.

This above-mentioned self-stimulation by means of my consciousness began to take place in me as a result of experiencing in all my Being a peculiar feeling, a mixture of " self-satisfaction " and " pride ", which arose in me every time I made accidental or half-foreseen verifications in the course of my further investigations of ever new and new facts concerning people's lives in general, facts about the existence of which I had never found a hint either in daily life or in my readings, although I had read almost everything existing about these questions in contemporary literature, as well as all the material from the past surviving until our day,—a literature accessible to me because of quite accidental circumstances of my life in a quantity far beyond the usual possibilities of the ordinary man.

Until that year I did not succeed in discovering anything, anywhere or from anybody, that could logically-and-harmoniously throw light upon even one aspect of this question, notwithstanding that, firstly, a restless factor reminding me automatically of the aim I had set myself was persistently active in my Being in almost every psychic state ; secondly, Great Nature had benevolently provided all my family and me in particular—and that not only in my opinion but in that of a great many people with whom I came in contact—with the highest degree of comprehension attainable by man ; thirdly, from childhood I had, among other capabilities, one especially developed,—that of eliciting from people their most sacred aims and intentions ; and fourthly, I had, in accordance with the peculiar conditions of my life, the possibility of gaining access to the so-called '' holy-of-holies '' of nearly all hermetic organizations such as religious, philosophical, occult, political and mystic societies, congregations, parties, unions etc., which were inaccessible to the ordinary man, and of discussing and exchanging views with innumerable people who, in comparison with others, are real authorities.

Although I did not succeed until this period in elucidating anything, I never lost hope that somewhere, and at some time, I should finally meet people who would explain to me or at least direct my state of mind to corresponding thoughts and considerations, which would help me to resolve for myself clearly and satisfactorily this, for me, fateful question.

Living in this way until that year, that is, absorbing

all external impressions and experiencing them inwardly in connection almost only with this mania of mine, and outwardly occupying myself with all kinds of professions and handicrafts to the end, on the one hand, of obtaining means of livelihood and, on the other, of mastering, according to the capacity inherent in me since childhood, every possible kind of human craft as yet unknown to me, but chiefly to the end of adapting myself in a more or less corresponding way to the particular conditions of the moment, conditions which I frequently changed in order to realize this inner aim of mine, I arrived then, in the above-mentioned year, at the definite conclusion that it would be utterly impossible to find out what I was looking for among my contemporaries and therefore decided one day to abandon everything and to retire for a definite period into complete isolation, away from all manifestations of the outer world, and to endeavour by means of active reflections to attain to this myself or to think out some new ways for my fertile researches.

This took place during my stay in Central Asia, when, thanks to the introduction of a street-barber, whom I accidentally met and with whom I became great friends, I happened to obtain access into a monastery well known among the followers of the Mahometan religion, and I availed myself of the hospitality of the good brothers.

Once, after a talk with some of the brothers of this monastery about the nature and quality of human faith, and the consequences of the action of its impulse on man, I, under the influence of this discourse, became still further convinced that I must abide by my decision and profit immediately by this opportunity in this very monastery.

Retiring into isolation that very evening, I put myself into the necessary state and began seriously meditating upon my situation and future conduct.

Following the necessary and, to me, already familiar method customary to all initiates in that branch of ancient science called " the-laws-of-contemplation ", consisting, in the given case, chiefly in the remembering and reviewing all the already existing categorical convictions on this subject, I began to confront different facts I personally had fully conceived with all kinds of hypotheses and conjectures I had heard from different authoritative people who, compared with others, were possessed of really great knowledge, and had also attained to a state of being corresponding to this knowledge.

As a result of pursuing this method for three days, while I did not arrive at any definite conclusions, I still became clearly and absolutely convinced that the answers for which I was looking, and which in their totality might throw light on this cardinal question of mine, can only be found, if they are at all accessible to man, in the sphere of " man's-subconscious-mentation ".

Then I became firmly convinced also that, for this purpose, it was indispensable for me to perfect my knowledge of all the details of the formation as well as of the mechanism of the manifestation of man's general psyche.

Arriving at this categorical conclusion, I began again, for several days and in my habitual manner, to think and think almost uninterruptedly about what should be done in order to create requisite and satisfactory worldly conditions making possible the study of such an unexpected problem.

Still completely a slave of these deliberations, I left the monastery and took up my wanderings again, this time with no definite plan of action.

During these uninterrupted peregrinations of mine from place to place, and almost continuous and intense

19

reflection about this, I at last formed a preliminary plan in my mind.

Liquidating all my affairs and mobilizing all my material and other possibilities, I began to collect all kinds of written literature and oral information, still surviving among certain Asiatic peoples, about that branch of science, which was highly developed in ancient times and called " Mehkeness ", a name signifying the " taking-away-of-responsibility ", and of which contemporary civilisation knows but an insignificant portion under the name of " hypnotism ", while all the literature extant upon the subject was already as familiar to me as my own five fingers.

Collecting all I could, I went to a certain Dervish monastery, situated likewise in Central Asia and where I had already stayed before, and, settling down there, I devoted myself wholly to the study of the material in my possession.

After two years of thorough theoretical study of this branch of science, when it became necessary to verify practically certain indispensable details, not as yet sufficiently elucidated by me in theory, of the mechanism of the functioning of man's subconscious sphere, I began to give myself out to be a " healer " of all kinds of vices and to apply the results of my theoretical studies to them, affording them at the same time, of course, real relief.

This continued to be my exclusive preoccupation and manifestation for four or five years in accordance with the essential oath imposed by my task, which consisted in rendering conscientious aid to sufferers, in never using my knowledge and practical power in that domain of science except for the sake of my investigations, and never for personal or egotistical ends, I not only arrived at unprecedented practical results without equal in our day, but also elucidated almost everything necessary for me.

In a short time, I discovered many details which might contribute to the solution of the same cardinal question, as well as many secondary facts, the existence of which I had scarcely suspected.

At the same time, I also became convinced that the greater number of minor details necessary for the final elucidation of this question must be sought not only in the sphere of man's subconscious mentation, but in various aspects of the manifestations in his state of waking consciousness.

After establishing this definitely, thoughts again began from time to time to " swarm " in my mind, as they had done years ago, sometimes automatically, sometimes directed by my consciousness,—thoughts as to the means of adapting myself now to the conditions of ordinary life about me with a view to elucidating finally and infallibly this question, which obviously had become a lasting and inseparable part of my Being.

This time my reflections, which recurred periodically during the two years of my wanderings on the continents of Asia, Europe and Africa, resulted in a decision to make use of my exceptional, for the modern man, knowledge of the so-called " supernatural sciences ", as well as of my skill in producing different " tricks " in the domain of these so-called " sciences ", and to give myself out to be, in these pseudo-scientific domains, a so-called " professor-instructor ".

It must be said that the main reason for this decision was my realisation of the fact that, at that time, there was, among men, a widely prevalent and specific psychosis which, as has been long established, attains periodically a high degree and is manifested by people giving themselves up to various " woeful " ideas in these spheres of quasi-human knowledge, which, in different epochs, bore different names, and which today are called " occultism ", " theosophism ", " spiritualism ", etc.

From the moment of this decision I directed all my capacities and attention to coming into contact with people belonging to one or other of these vast organizations, where people foregathered in an attempt to reach certain special results by studying one sort or another of the above-mentioned " sciences ".

The ensuing circumstances of my life were so favourable to me that, within six months, I succeeded not only in coming into contact with a great number of these people, but even in being accepted as a well known " expert " and guide in evoking so-called " phenomena-of-the-beyond " in a very large " circle ", as they called it.

After I had been " acclimatised " to my new calling, my reputation among all the members of the aforesaid " circle " and even among their families became that of a great " maestro " in all that comprised supernatural knowledge. At the time of these so-called " manipulations " in the realm of the beyond, which I performed in the presence of a large number of members of one of the numerous, widespread, then as today upon Earth, " workshops-for-the-perfection-of-psychopathism ", a name I now openly call them, I began to observe and study various manifestations in the waking state of the psyche of these trained and freely moving " Guinea-Pigs ", allotted to me by Destiny for my experiments.

Although by the beginning of the third year of this activity I had already acquired a solid authority among the members of three such large independent " Workshops ", through which I obtained a great deal of material for my observations, and in spite of the fact that I could have had as many as I wanted, I was compelled to give them all up and to undertake the organization of my own " circle " on quite new principles, with a staff of people chosen specially by me.

I decided to do so mainly for the reason that, meeting then a great number of people usually composing such circles, I had elucidated and established the fact that in such societies foregather generally people of three or four definite " types ", whereas it was necessary for me —in order to observe the manifestations of man's psyche in his waking state—to have at my disposal representatives of all the 28 " categories-of-types " existing on Earth, as they were established in ancient times.

Putting this plan into execution with enormous and almost superhuman effort, and with, of course, very heavy expenditure, I organized, in different cities, three small groups of people of as varying types as I could possibly muster in the course of three years.

Realising during the second year of the existence of these groups organized by me that, under the prevailing conditions, I would not be able to have at my disposal, for a period long enough for my observations, the representatives of all the types, and while continuing to direct these groups, on the one hand, observing and studying the material already available, and, on the other, satisfying as conscientiously as possible those in whose psyche the passion of curiosity was deeply rooted, and impartially destroying in those others, in whom the predisposition proper to all men for acquiring a real " Being " was not yet atrophied, all their former illusions and erroneous ideals, in this way preparing, in all events, possible assistants for me in the future, I began periodically to ponder again in order to find still the possibility of creating such conditions as would allow me to satisfy at last this

23

extraordinary and accidentally roused need of mine.

These periodical deliberations finally led me to found the Institute, which later existed under the name of the **" Institute - For - Man's - Harmonious - Develop - ment-**according-to-the-system-of-**G. Gurdjieff ".**

The " canvas ", so to say, which served as a background for this decision was the consideration that, with such a broadly planned public organization, embracing as it did almost all the interests of contemporary life, I would be sure to bring together—apart from the types I had mainly met before—all the other types of people previously lacking for my observations.

Setting forth in this booklet the motives for my decision at that time, based as it was upon inner, sincere and impartial impulses, I consider it necessary to speak of the mental and emotive associations flowing through my entirety and which, in their sum-total, gave rise to this decision, which was in complete harmony with my conscience.

Towards the end of all my reflections at that time, as a result of which I had at last firmly decided to organize such a public Institute, when there arose in my entirety then, as has always happened in similar cases, that strange impulse which is proper to my peculiar individuality and which automatically compels me to consider always each new task in life also from the point of view of " objective justice ", my reasonings with myself were as follows :

" To make use of people, who display a special interest in an Institute founded by me, for purely personal ends would surely strike those around me as a manifestation of " egotism ", but at the same time the people, who had anything to do with such an Institute established by me, those, namely, whom I have previously mentioned and in whom the predisposition proper to all men,—that of acquiring data and of preparing in their being the soil for the impulse of " objective-conscience " and for the formation of so-called " essential-prudence "—had not yet entirely atrophied, could, in this way alone, profit by the results of knowledge amassed by me due to exceptional circumstances of my life, and which had regard to nearly all the aspects of reality and objective truth, and thus use them for their own benefit. "

As to the location of this Institute, I decided, after a great deal of deliberation and after taking into account the existing circumstances of ordinary life and the facilities of intercourse with other nations so essential to me, that the most suitable place would be Russia, which at that time was peaceful, rich and quiet.

Arriving at this final decision, I began at once to liquidate my " current " affairs, which were dispersed over different countries in Asia, and collecting all the wealth which I had amassed during my long life, which was an exceptionally laborious one for a modern man, I came and settled in the very heart of Russia, in the City of Moscow.

This happened two years before the so-called " Great-World-War ".

In this booklet I shall not say anything more about this Institute, which I first founded in Russia, where the unexpected and catastrophic events of the World War destroyed it at the very height of its earlier activities and with it all the results hitherto obtained. I shall not describe also the further " peripeteias " or the attempts to organize such an Institute again in various other towns in Russia, as well as in other countries, attempts which all came to nothing because of all the various consequences of the War and each time with a " crash " involving enormous material and other loss; and its fundamental and successful establishment seven years later in noble

25

France, where it existed without hindrance until its general liquidation following my serious motor-accident.

I shall not speak about these events and all the consequences flowing from them, because I have already described them in sufficient detail, partly in the third book of the second series of my writings, and partly in the first book of the third series.

From the material which refers to this Institute then founded by me, I shall now quote only certain passages from the " prospectus " announcing the opening of this Institute.

I should like to quote these passages principally because, as I clearly understood later upon becoming acquainted with the life of European people, this prospectus, though circulated everywhere in great numbers, still remains unknown to the majority of European people. And the majority had not even had the opportunity of becoming acquainted with it because, in my opinion, my work and ideas greatly interested, from the very beginning, such people as were already in the highest degree " possessed " of the before-mentioned " specific-psychosis " and were accordingly known to those around them as being preoccupied with every kind of " nonsense ", otherwise known under such names as " occultism ", " theosophism ", " Anthroposophism ", " psychoanalysis ", and so on, and when any, who had not as yet come under the influence of such " nonsense ", came into contact with anything touching my activity and discovered that Mr. So and So was very interested in this activity, there immediately arose in their psyche that " something ", which is proper to man's psyche in his collective life and which was recorded long ago by our ancestors and called the " buffer-of-prejudice ".

I shall begin by quoting that part of the prospectus

which gives, among other things, an estimate of man's education in contemporary civilisation. It says :

" Contemporary man, owing to certain, almost imperceptible conditions of ordinary life which are firmly rooted in modern civilisation and which seem to have become, so to speak, " inevitable " in daily life, has gradually deviated from the natural type he ought to have represented on account of the sum-total of the influences of place and environment in which he was born and reared and which, under normal conditions, without any artificial impediments, would have indicated by their very nature for each individual the lawful path of his development in that final normal type which he ought to have become even in his preparatory age.

Today, civilisation, with its unlimited scope in extending its influence, has wrenched man from the normal conditions in which he should be living.

It is, of course, true that modern civilisation has opened up for man new and vaster horizons in different technical, mechanical and many other so-called " sciences ", thereby enlarging his world perception, but civilisation has, instead of a balanced rising to a higher degree of development, developed only certain sides of his general being to the detriment of others, while, because of the absence of an harmonious education, certain faculties inherent in man have even been completely destroyed, depriving him in this way of the natural privileges of his type. In other words, by not educating the growing generation harmoniously, this civilisation, which should have been, according to common sense, in all respects like a good mother to man, has withheld from him what she should have given him ; and, it appears, that she has even taken from him the possibility of the progressive and balanced development of a new type, which development would have inevitably

27

taken place if only in the course of time and according to the law of general human progress.

From this follows the indubitable fact, which can be clearly established, that, instead of an accomplished individual type, which historical data would show man to have been some centuries ago and one normally in communion with Nature and the environment generating him, there developed instead a being that was uprooted from the soil, unfit for life, and a stranger to all normal conditions of existence.

One of the most pernicious results of a one-sided education is that the perceptions and manifestations of the modern man, who becomes finally formed in responsible age, are not the conscious expression of his Being as a complete whole, but represent only the results of automatic reflexes of one or another part of his general entirety.

The general psyche of the modern man is split into three, so to say, completely independent " entities ", which bear no relation to each other and which are separate both in their functions and in their manifestations, whereas, according to historical data, these three sources formed, in the majority of people, even in the time of the Babylonian civilisation, one indivisible whole, which appeared to be at once a common repository of all their perceptions and the radiating Centre of their manifestations.

Because of this one-sided education of the modern man, upon the attainment of his majority, these three entirely independent sources or centres of his life, that is, firstly, the source of his intellectual life, secondly, the source of his " emotional " life, and, thirdly, his instinct or " motor " centre, instead of fusing inwardly in the normal way to produce common outer manifestations, have become, especially of late, quite independent outward functions, and not only the methods of education of those functions, but also the quality of their manifestations, have become dependent on special outer subjective conditions.

According to the deductions based on detailed experiments made by Mr. Gurdjieff himself, as well as those by many other people who have seriously thought about this question, every really conscious perception and manifestation of man can only result from the simultaneous and co-ordinate working of the three aforesaid sources, which make up his general individuality, and each of which must fulfil its role, that is, furnish its own share of associations and experiences.

The complete achievement of the requisite and normal manifestation in each distinct case is possible only upon the co-ordination of the activity of all these three sources.

In the modern man, partly owing to his abnormal education during his preparatory age, and partly owing to influences due to certain causes of the generally established abnormal conditions of modern life, the working of his psychic centres during his responsible age is almost entirely disconnected, therefore his intellectual, emotional and instinctive motor functions do not serve as a natural complement and corrective for one another, but, on the contrary, travel along different roads, which rarely meet and for this reason permit very little leisure for obtaining that, which should in reality be understood by the word " consciousness ", wrongly used by modern people today.

As a result of the lack of co-ordinated activity on the part of these three separately formed and independently educated parts of man's general psyche, it has come about that a modern man represents three different men in a single individual ; the first of whom thinks in complete isolation from the other parts, the second merely feels, and the third acts only automatically, according to established or accidental reflexes of his organic functions.

These three men in one should, in accordance with the foresight of Great Nature, represent, taken together in responsible age, one man as he ought to be : the " man-without-inverted-commas ", that is, the real man.

These three, who were deliberately shaped by Great Nature to compose one complete whole, as a consequence of not assuming at the right time the habit of mutual understanding and aid, through the fault of men themselves and of their false education, produce this result that, in the period of responsible manifestations of the modern man, they not only never help one another, but are, on the contrary, automatically compelled to frustrate the plans and intentions of each other ; moreover, each of them, by dominating the others in moments of intensive action, appears to be the master of the situation, in this way falsely assuming the responsibilities of the real " I ".

This realisation of disconnected and conflicting activity of the centres of origin, which ought to represent the psyche of man, and, at the same time, of the complete absence of even a theoretical conception of the indispensability of an education corresponding to these separate, relatively independent parts, setting aside the ignorance of its practical application, must inevitably lead to the conclusion that man is not master even of himself.

He cannot be master of himself, for not only does he not control these centres, which ought to function in complete subordination to his consciousness, but he does not even know which of his centres governs them all.

The system applied in the **Institute For Man's Harmo-**

nious Development for observing human psychic activities clearly demonstrates that the modern man never acts of his own accord, but only manifests actions stimulated by external irritations.

The modern man does not think, but something thinks for him ; he does not act, but something acts through him ; he does not create, but something is created through him ; he does not achieve, but something is achieved through him.

In a newly-born child these three diverse parts of the general human psyche may be compared to a system of blank gramophone rolls upon which begin to be recorded, from the day of its appearance into the world, the external significance of objects and the subjective understanding of their inner significance, or the sense of the results of all actions taking place in the outer world, as well as in the inner world already forming in him ; all this is recorded in accordance with the correspondence between the nature of these actions and the nature of those distinct systems which form themselves in man.

All kinds of these recorded results of environing actions remain unchanged on each of these " depository-rolls " for life, in the same sequence and in the same correlation with the impressions previously recorded, in which they are perceived.

All the impressions recorded in these three relatively independent parts, composing man's general psyche, later produce, in the period of responsible age, all kinds of associations in diverse combinations.

That which is called " reason " in man, as well as in all other external forms of life, is nothing more than the concentration of the results of impressions of different quality formerly perceived ; and the stimulation and repetition of the se provokes different kinds of associations in the being.

31

The recorded impressions have three sources of origin, and are subject to three different law-abiding influences.

One category of associations is formed by impressions perceived involuntarily and coming directly from the outer world as well as springing from man's inner world, as a result of certain previous, constant and automatically repeated associations.

The second category is formed by voluntarily perceived impressions either springing from the external world or crystallising in man's inner world by means of deliberate active thinking and verifications of reality.

And the third category originates exclusively from the process of so-called " transformed-contemplation ", that is, from the confrontation of homogeneous impressions of all origins, which were already fixed, while continuous contact is maintained between their inner and separate centres.

The depositing in man's entirety of the three distinct categories of impressions, enumerated above, for the subsequent manifestations of man's general psyche confirms, among other things, the real diversity of the three determinate states of man's consciousness and defines their quality and importance.

By the methods of the **Institute For Man's Harmonious Development** one can quite definitely, and without the slightest doubt, establish that man's consciousness is made up of three definite capacities of manifestation, and these capacities are formed of and are determined by the associations of impressions which have their origin in one of the three above-mentioned categories.

One of the three states of consciousness, which, in the objective sense, is considered the highest and most desirable for man, reposes exclusively on associations of previously perceived impressions of the third category only.

The second state of consciousness is made up of the associations of impressions of the second order mentioned above, that is, of those voluntarily perceived.

To the third state of human consciousness can be attributed, without any difficulty, the kind of consciousness for which the modern man, in his desire to emphasize its great importance and never doubting the correctness of his denomination, has adopted the expression of the " waking-state-of-consciousness ".

This state of consciousness, which modern man ranks highest, has, according to scientifically organized and carefully verified experimental elucidations, proved to be the product of constantly repeated, involuntarily and accidentally perceived, as well as of artificially created and " learnt-by-rote ", impressions.

The majority of people today, as a consequence of the continually deteriorating conditions of their normal existence, have become accustomed to give priority to this consciousness, which is attained by the impressions just mentioned, that is, by the " learnt-by-rote ", involuntary perceptions of accidental impressions received from our environment.

In the man who attains his highest degree of consciousness by means of associations, composed of impressions of the first kind, the processes of imagination, memory, judgment, reasoning and thinking, are no more than an automatic crystallisation, resulting from his so-called " concentrated efforts ", which process he calls by the high-sounding name of " attention ", whereas these already crystallised and automatically perceived impressions, and all the aforesaid manifestations, are nothing more than the result of previously repeated and accidental impressions, in other words all the processes of this man's inner world are only an automatic reviewing in various combinations of the oft repeated experiences of, so to speak, " antiquated " impressions. And this man's manifestations in ordinary life, all his impulses, thoughts, feelings, words, convictions, beliefs and deeds, are made up exclusively from the material of such impressions in their various combinations, crystallised in his entirety.

And these combinations are formed under the influence of chance shocks which set in motion more or less intensively one or another group of previously perceived impressions, which, in the given case, become the centre of associations.

Each new shock, or a shock of a different degree of intensity, evokes yet another association and, consequently, another train of thought, feeling and action, etc., and no centre in the possesser of such a consciousness can add anything of its own or anything new to the combinations thus formed, nor can the centre, even when acting at its moment of greatest intensity, draw on the material formed in other centres.

It follows that, as the world perception of the possesser of such a consciousness is always come by only by one part of him or, in other words, as the possesser of such a consciousness has three diverse processes of perception, which have but little in common or associate by chance and only partially, each of his judgments, as the product of one part only of his psyche and the expressions of a part of the material at his disposal, is invariably one-sided and, as a result, necessarily erroneous.

From what has just been said it must be obvious to every sane-thinking person that the first task necessary for the real education of man is to develop in each separately formed centre the natural need to blend simultaneously the functions of one part with the others, in order that the manifestations of these three parts, formed separately according to the laws of nature in man's general psyche, and which inevitably demand a separate education, may be harmoniously united, and may, in the period of responsible life, work together according to their normal capacities.

Only this attitude in the preparing of man for responsible life can bring the different sources composing man's general psyche to the same level of manifestation, as only then will the three principal wheels of the human machine work smoothly, without hindrance to their mutual work and yield the highest degree of productivity in their separate functioning, as well as in the attainment of that level of consciousness attainable by man but which man never reaches under ordinary conditions.

Taking into consideration that the degree of development in each individual of each part of his whole individuality differs, and that his associations likewise differ, we are forced to the conclusion that the work of educating and re-educating each person must be strictly individual and cannot be otherwise.

All the faults in the functioning of the human machine, due to the conditions of ordinary life, increase with time, and any repairs of the machine at work can only be obtained by a constant and determined struggle against all the resulting defects.

Based on the so-called " experimental-material " handed down from the past together with the numerous elucidations made today by the **Institute For Man's Harmonious Development,** it is already categorically established that man is unable to carry on by himself the aforesaid struggle. Again it will not help him to work on himself by any of the various methods of self-training and self-development which have lately become widespread in the world and which recommend definite methods and processes, such as various physical exercises, exercises in meditation and concentration, breathing exercises, various systems of diet, fasting, etc., for all and sundry.

To apply such methods to everyone, without taking into account individual needs and peculiarities, is not only useless but can even become dangerous; for ignorant attempts at repairing the machine, while effecting certain changes, unavoidably cause other and unnecessary changes, which an inexperienced and ignorant person can neither foresee nor guard against.

One must always be aware that the human machine, whether functioning regularly or irregularly, is in itself always in mechanical equilibrium and, consequently, any change in one direction is bound to bring about a change in another direction, and it is therefore absolutely essential to foresee and counter this.

In order to avoid undesirable results and unexpected consequences in working upon one's self, it is necessary to submit to the discipline of special and strictly individual methods, aimed at the development of new and particular " inertias ", by means of which, under the direction of an experienced guide, the old ones may be regulated and altered, in other words, it is necessary to develop new faculties, which are unattainable in ordinary life, and which man can neither develop unaided nor by the help of any general method.

In this precisely consist the principal characteristics of the method adopted by the Institute For - Man's - Harmonious - Development - according - to - the - system - of-G. Gurdjieff, that it leads to the discovery of hitherto undeveloped faculties in man, faculties which are essential for his responsible and relatively normal life.

To this end, and keeping in mind its verified possibilities, the programme of the Institute For Man's Harmonious Development includes the practical application of a special " line-of-work ", from which a careful choice of some definite type of work is made for every person, according to his individual capacities,—work which corresponds with those parts of his abnormally constructed psyche, the automatic activity of which has to be developed or diminished.

To the same end, this programme includes a medical section, since, for many people, it is necessary, before undertaking the development of their natural capacities, to correct first of all the already existent functional disorders, without which it is impossible to achieve productive work aimed at the desired harmonious development.

Keeping in mind what has just been said, one must note that any work for the self-perfection of man can be useful only when the direction is grounded upon a thorough knowledge of human nature, and is in strict accordance with the individual determining of the physical and psychic properties of the person, as well as the circumstances and conditions of his external life in the future, as far as they can be predicted.

Therefore special courses are selected from the subjects included in the programme of the Institute and are adapted to the individual needs of each pupil.

The study, by special methods, of different trades, handicrafts, arts and domestic sciences, is included in the programme of the Institute.

Parallel to this, a thorough theoretical study is pursued of man and the world in all their inner-relations and according to the data of European science, as well as of ancient Asiatic knowledge.

Such a study, which demands the application of new and unusual methods of perception and thought assists, on the one hand, the development of the hidden properties in man, and, on the other, contributes to the establishment of a correct process of thought and feeling, as well as of requisite automatic actions.

The Institute For Man's Harmonious Development includes, among its principal instructors, specialists in medicine, psychology, physiology, physico-mathematical sciences, handicrafts and all kinds of physical and psychic exercises.

These intructors, besides being trained in their special fields, are fully initiated into that branch of science of which fragments have always existed in the life of man, and which is now being worked out by Mr. Gurdjieff, with all the changes and additions corresponding with the particular circumstances crystallized in contemporary life, and serves as the basis for his Institute.

The Institute accepts adults of both sexes up to 60 years of age and children over 4 years of age.

People entering the Institute are divided into three categories :

The first includes persons aiming at self-development in accordance with a programme specially drawn up for them.

The second includes persons, who pursue the methods of the Institute with a view to studying one or another subject of their choice ; also those persons who seek to be cured by the methods of the Institute.

The third includes persons who attend only the general lectures and study one special subject indicated for them by the Institute *.

---

* Certain subjects of the lectures as well as of the practical programme are given only to pupils of the first category.

People of the first category will in the future, as is prescribed, be divided into three groups, called :

1) **the Exoteric group.**
2) **the Mesoteric group.**
and 3) **the Esoteric group.**

All newly admitted pupils of the first category belong at the beginning to the " Exoteric " group ; later they should, according to personal merit, pass into the " Mesoteric " group, and then, again according to merit and to the degree of " comprehension ", pass into the " Esoteric " group.

Only after passing through all three groups can they be initiated, first theoretically, and then practically, into all the questions which are unknown to ordinary people and which have been elucidated by Mr. Gurdjieff himself in the course of his special researches of almost half a century, as well as by a group of people of the highest contemporary culture who have wholly devoted themselves to the research of objective truth.

Those of the first category receive, when entering the Institute, definite directions and indications only after filling out completely the paragraphs of the so-called " individual-record ", which is made for each person separately.

The material given in this " individual-record " will indicate the detailed observations of the principal functions of his organism and the specific traits of each given subject crystallized in his individuality, as well as the degree of attention, memory, speech, sense of combination, temperament, the form of his physical and psychic reflexes, smell, taste, hearing, sight, reaction to colours, quality of emanation, etc.

The results of these observations, together with the

various data elucidated during the same period as to the capacities and inclinations of the given individual and marked down on the " individual record ", will be the " starting-point ", so to speak, for the instructors for establishing a method of productive self-development. On the basis of the same data a choice of subjects to be studied will be indicated, as well as a graduated plan of special psychic work, a corresponding mode of life while in the Institute, and, in cases of illness, the necessary cure.

Particular attention will be paid to those individuals who show certain pathological symptoms, such as weakness of will, " wilfulness ", laziness, unreasonable fears, a sense of continual fatigue, apathy, irritability, irregular exchange of substances, obesity or exhaustion, abuse of alcohol, narcotics, etcetera.

There has been installed in the main section of the Institute the most modern apparatus and instruments, a collection richer than any ever heard of on Earth before, if we look on it as on the assembling in one place of " physico-metric " and " chemico-analytic ", " psycho-experimental " cabinets, serving requirements of a general character and also for independent investigation by the pupils themselves, in order that they might verify such theories and the statements propounded in general lectures as may appear doubtful or abitrary to them ".

Returning to the main subject of this booklet, I wish to state, first of all, that this Institute, after innumerable trials, was more or less set up and finally established by me in France in 1921, upon the principles of the above-mentioned prospectus. But it did not survive long, not only to my great sorrow, but, as many will probably understand, to the misfortune of all thinking people, for, although my activity followed at first chiefly what may appear as my personal aim, I foresaw very soon all the profit it might bring to all humanity, and developed it on a scale to interest and to embrace the entire, so-called, " sanethinking-world ".

At the height of its activity, on account of my motor-accident, already known to many, and which brought me near to death, I was forced to liquidate not only everything prepared for the opening activity in various countries of 18 new sections of the Institute, but also everything immediately connected with the main section.

I shall not describe in this booklet what events came to pass as a consequence of the catastrophe which befell me and what unexpected circumstances derived from all this, circumstances compelling me as soon as I completely recovered consciousness to take all measures for liquidating everything as soon as possible that had been created by me with such unimagined efforts, as it has been already expounded in detail in one of the books of the third series.

From all that I have already said about this, I shall repeat, in this given case, only in brief the main reasons which obliged me at that time to begin writing and even to become finally a " standard writer ".

Some months after the above-mentioned motor-accident, when I myself, and all the people near me, became certain that I would live, and when all the former crystallised functions and the established tempo of the intensive activity of my spirit began, day by day, to be more and more re-established, while my physical body still remained quite helpless, thus producing disharmony between the state of my body and my spirit, and making me very often experience moral sufferings, I decided to find for myself an occupation which would give my thoughts another direction and thus diminish these moral sufferings.

One night, while still in bed and suffering from the insomnia which was habitual to me at that time, stirred by association, and remembering a thought concerning a plan which, during the last two or three months, had always perturbed me and finally even obsessed me,—and which should have been realised at the time when I drew up the general scheme of means for attaining the afore-said fundamental aim of all my life, which included the intention to spread the essence of my ideas also by means of literature, and which failed on account of the untrustworthiness and vicious idleness of those people whom I had specially prepared during many years for that specific purpose,—it suddenly occurred to me that there was no reason why I should not take advantage of the present situation and should not begin to dictate myself the material for the realisation of this aim.

Consequently, continuing to ponder, I finally decided that I would do so.

The following evening I asked one of the people near me to take a pencil and notebook and to write down exactly all that I would dictate.

At first, intending to spread the different aspects of my ideas in the form of short scenarios suitable for theatre or cinema, I dictated at the beginning such scenarios, and began to " bake " every other day a fresh and com-pleted scenario.

I shall mention only four of the numerous scenarios dictated by me :

" **The Cocainists** ".
" **The Chiromancy of the Stock-Exchange** ".
" **The Unconscious Murder** ".
" **The Three Brothers** ".

To give at least an approximate idea of the character

of these, so to speak, small " literary compositions ", which I dictated then, and which will also become known to the public in due time, and the subjects of which were often formed in my mind under the influence of this or that impression on my organs of perception, which at that period were particularly sensitive, I find it sufficient to speak here about an event which inspired me to express certain thoughts derived from my ideas, in the last of the above-mentioned scenarios, entitled " The Three Bro-thers ".

Some weeks after I had begun my dictation, when this new occupation not only contributed to put an end to the concentration of my thoughts on my desperate state and on the situation from which I saw no way out, but soon took on the character of a " not-to-be-trifled-with " enthusiasm, and, in the end, resulted in the re-establishment of the disharmonised functions of my physical body which proceeded in an accelerated tempo, I decided, although I could not yet move alone, in order to rest from active thinking and to obtain generally a change of impressions, to go to Paris by car, accompanied by some of the people close to me.

Sitting one evening, during one of these visits, in the Café de la Paix, famous then for foreigners, with some friends, we were discussing all kinds of questions.

Among other things was mentioned a film, popular at that time, called " Two-Brothers ", and one of my companions suggested that we should go and see this famous film, which was being shown at a cinema specially arranged for it.

We all decided to go and, as the cinema was quite near, I walked to it, although with great difficulty.

There was an incredible crush in the cinema, the tickets were difficult to get, but one of my companions managed to get hold of some, paying, apparently, an " astronomical " sum.

I do not consider it necessary to repeat here the contents of that nonsense, which was the " pick " of the season, but I must say that sitting in that room overcrowded with people who, on account of bad ventilation were obliged to breathe bad air, I, unable to get out, was compelled willynilly to look at the film, and to look intensely, for the focus of my sight was not yet re-established, and I had to fix the various objects sometimes with one eye and sometimes with the other, and the whole time I felt revolted by such senseless " fashionable bluff ", the popularity of which was due entirely to the herd-instinct, especially prevalent among people today.

At the close of this, what I should call, " general hypnotic-process ", in order to fix firmly some formerly suggested ideas, I, " hobbling " and supported by my companions, returned to the Café de la Paix, which later became my Paris " office ", and regaining gradually my calm, began to form in my mind the outline of the scenario which I have called " The Three-Brothers ".

In this scenario three brothers act instead of two, and all their manifestations and inter-relations are compared by me to the manifestations and inter-relations of the three separate, independently formed and relatively educated parts of man's general entirety, representing, in fact, firstly, the physical, secondly, the astral, and thirdly, the mental body of man ; and, in the dialogues of the three characters, in the form of a discussion, that is, affirming and denying, I introduced certain ideas which have come down to us from ancient times, when the science of medicine was very highly developed, ideas of what is useful or harmful, satisfactory or unsatisfactory for one or other

of the characters of the scenario in the process of transforming of this or that substance.

During the first two or three months, obliged to dictate
owing to my weakness, I set forth, without a definite
system, ideas taken separately from the general totality,
—fragments, in the form of small scenarios, representing
various external episodes in the lives of different people.

But later on, when my physical strength was more or
less re-established, I began to write myself ; and then,
during the reading aloud of one of these scenarios of
mine, the subject of which was a legend I had heard in
childhood about the appearance, of the first human beings
on Earth and of which I had made Beelzebub, as a likely
witness of this appearance, the principal hero, I perceived
in that scenario a very rich source from which might
be extracted numberless corresponding points of departure
for an easy comprehension of explanations of various
facets of my ideas, and decided, therefore, to cease writing small scenarios and to write a master-work, taking
this scenario as the foundation for all my further writings.

From that time on, exploiting to the full this source
for a logical development of one or another of the questions, which, in their totality, might provide a clear understanding of the essence of my ideas, I began to expound
and elaborate all the material beforehand selected for
publication, following this time a definite system.

Since then, during all those years, until today, I occupied
myself exclusively with writing, and often, on account
of new plans which suggested themselves in the course of
my meditations, I changed the text, as well as the outward
form, of what was already written, and only last year
did I finally adopt the text and the final form in which
my writings will be published.

To give the reader immediately, in this booklet, an idea

of this finally selected form of all my writings, and at the same time not to strain again my poor brain, which is already tired out, I shall simply give here the first six title-pages of the writings of my first book, which is completely finished and given to the printer.

G. GURDJIEFF.

ALL AND EVERYTHING

*Ten books
in three series.*

The original is written in Russian and Armenian. Translations into other languages have been and are still being made under the personal direction of the author himself by a group of translators specially trained in conformity with their defined individuality, and chosen according to their understanding of the text of what is translated, and the philological peculiarities of each language.

PARIS.

1933.

Everything is expounded according to new principles of logical understanding with the purpose of solving three cardinal problems.

PROBLEM
OF THE FIRST SERIES.

Mercilessly, without any compromise whatsoever, to extirpate from the mentation and feeling of man the previous, century-rooted views and beliefs about everything existing in the world.

PROBLEM
OF THE SECOND SERIES.

To furnish the material required for a new creation and to prove its soundness and good quality.

PROBLEM
OF THE THIRD SERIES.

To contribute to the arising in the mentation and feeling of man of an authentic and correct representation of the World existing in reality and not that illusory one, which, according to the affirmation and proof of the author is perceived by all people.

FIRST SERIES

In three books under the common title of

" AN OBJECTIVELY-IMPARTIAL CRITICISM OF THE LIFE OF MAN "

or

" BEELZEBUB'S TALES TO HIS GRANDSON ".

————

SECOND SERIES

In three books under the common title of

" MEETINGS WITH REMARKABLE MEN "

————

THIRD SERIES

In four books under the common title of

" LIFE IS REAL ONLY WHEN ' I AM ' ".

FIRST BOOK

of the series

" AN OBJECTIVELY-IMPARTIAL CRITICISM OF THE LIFE OF MAN "

or

" BEELZEBUB'S TALES TO HIS GRANDSON ".

Contents of the first series
first book.

Contents of second book.

Contents of third book.

A Friendly Counsel written impromptu by the author himself on delivering this book to the printer.

According to many deductions made by me during continuous experiments concerning the perception by contemporary people of new impressions from what is heard or read, as well as according to the sense of one saying of popular wisdom which I have just remembered and which has come down from ancient times to our very day formulated thus :

Every prayer may be heard by the Highest Forces And one might get a corresponding reward only if it is uttered thrice :

First—for the welfare or the peace of soul of one's parents ;

Second—for the welfare of one's neighbours ;

And only the third time—for one's own welfare.

I consider it necessary on the first page of this first book which is quite ready for publication to give the following advice :

Read each of my writings thrice :

First time—at least as you have already become mechanised to read all the contemporary books and magazines.

Second time—as if you were reading aloud to somebody else ;

And only the third time—try to grasp the gist of my writings.

Only then you may perhaps get your own impartial judgment peculiar to yourself about my writings and only then could be realised my hope that you, according to your understanding, would profit for yourself by the benefit which I assume and I wish you with all my being.

Signed AUTHOR.

Only now, having prepared, in my opinion, by means of everything already set forth in this booklet, a corresponding, so-to-say, " ground-work " for depicting before the inner eye of every reader different outlines of the essence of this booklet of mine, called by me " The-First-Appeal-To-Contemporary-Humanity ", I consider it right, before other things, to announce in the hearing of all that, although I undertake at last the publication of my writings, I have decided to promote their circulation not by the usual ways, but in accordance with a definite plan worked out by me.

This plan, newly formed by, me consists in taking all possible measures to prevent my writings, with the exception of the first series, from becoming at once property " accessible-to-everybody ".

This decision of mine, made during the last years in the course of my observations of those who listened to the readings of my current work, is the result of long consideration, and is a conclusion contrary to my original hope of the possibility of making some more, generally available contribution to the healing of man's psyche, which has already become, during the last centuries, almost completely abnormal.

In accordance with my decision I resolved to make accessible to the public only three books from the first series of my writings.

With regard to the books of the other two series, I intend to make known their contents in the following way :

The contents of the second series will be made known by means of readings, open to those who have already a thorough knowledge of the contents of the first series. These readings are intended to take place, in the meantime, in so-called circles already existent among many large groups of men which are made up of the followers of my ideas.

For this purpose, these already existing " circles ", access to which will be made much easier, will be re-organised and there will be opened " clubs " of quite a new type, easy of access, and in those places where there are no such " circles " there will be sent specially trained people to arrange readings.

Acquaintance with the contents of the third series of my writings is permitted only to those people who, besides having a thorough knowledge of the ideas exposed in the two previous series, have already begun to manifest themselves and to react to other people's manifestations in strict accordance with my indications set forth in the previous series of my writings.

The merit and proficiency of these people will be judged by some of those who have already been admitted to the so-called " rights-of-initiates ", according to the code established by me, or, as it might be better expressed, in accordance with the regulations modified by me, which have always existed on Earth among people who, in their search for truth, attained a certain definite Being.

Although I have taken all possible measures for the strict observance of this decision, I do not consider it vain to address a sincere appeal to all readers of my books to help me to the best of their ability in every way to carry out this decision, so that no one interested in my writings should ever attempt to read them in any other than the indicated order ; in other words, he should never read anything written by me before he is already well acquainted with the earlier works, even if someone, with a particular motive, should attempt to persuade him to commence the reading other than from the beginning.

Believe me, you must take my word for it, that the

exact carrying out of this wish of mine can be of great importance to you and your interests, and I, therefore, particularly stress and insist on it.

I shall not now write in detail of the consequences which will result if my request is not carried out ; these I have elucidated and verified by my own long observation and statistical calculations. I shall only say here that, for certain people, a reading of my writings in any other than the indicated order (no matter if the reader has long been a follower of my ideas or has become one recently), can provoke undesirable phenomena in their general psyche, one of which in particular might paralyse forever the possibility of normal self-perfection.

Now, in order to explain the plan of the publication of my writings, I have mentioned the people who have attained the " rights-of-initiates ", under whose guarantee others would be allowed to become acquainted with the ideas throwing light upon Truth and Reality in the third series ; and to evoke in the reader's mind even an approximative conception of these people and incidentally also of those under whose direction the common readings of the second series will take place, and in order to create, in this way, a right attitude towards them, I find it necessary to say this :

These two different categories of people, with whose co-operation I intend to make known to a wide public the contents of the second and third series of my writings, represent today the possessors of two quite different degrees of so-called " Being-and-Comprehension ".

The preparation for their future activity began as a result of two different circumstances which happened accidentally and were connected with my activity.

The circumstances which contributed to the formation of the first group of these people, who have to prove the worthiness of ordinary people for the right to become acquainted with the contents of the books of the third series of my writings, and who now will be my principal assistants in the new phase of my activity, were the following :

At the very beginning, when I had finally decided to organise the Institute on the principles mentioned already in this booklet, and was looking for a suitable country in which to put this into practice, I foresaw certain possible changes in the conditions of ordinary life and decided therefore, in any eventuality, to confide my intentions to a " brotherhood " (a kind of monastery existing in the very heart of Asia), with a view to securing in certain ways their future co-operation.

As a result of long discussions about all sorts of mutual obligations which, on my side, were chiefly on the grounds of my future religious and moral actions, and, on their side, were on the grounds of guiding, in strict accordance with the means indicated by me, the inner world of people whom I would confide to them, we came to a certain definite agreement.

And ever since, from 1911, when I arrived in the country which was then called " Russian-Turkestan ", and while moving from one town to another, towards Moscow, and coming into contact with different people answering my purpose while preparing everything necessary for the realization of my intentions, whenever I happened to meet, on the ground of my ideas, such people as had data corresponding to my purpose, which purpose was partly connected with my foreseen need of them in the future, I established relationship with them and, after the necessary mutual agreement and after supplying them with all needed, I sent them to that monastery.

During this entire period, and up to the time of my

aforesaid serious motor-accident, I travelled throughout the whole of Russia, the Caucasus, Turkey, Germany and England, to the place where I finally settled : hospitable France, meeting many tens of thousands of people from almost all the nations of Asia and Europe on the common ground of my ideas ; from whom I selected 27 of both sexes, answering in their data to my purpose, and sent them to the aforesaid monastery.

With the exception of three, one of whom was sent back on account of unworthy manifestations, after, of course, being put under a special " spell " of silence, so that he could not betray what he had seen or heard there, and two of whom died, one a victim of an hereditary disease and the other through an accident which occurred while he was searching for a medical plant, " Santchishook ", all the others, during the entire period, besides fulfilling all the established requirements of that monastery under the guidance of the elder brothers and of some of my former assistants, who paid me occasional visits in the " search-after-truth ", all of them reached a theoretical cognition in all of its details of the essence of the totality of my ideas, and assimilated it practically in their Being, with the aim of their own well merited objective good in their old age.

The circumstances, again very happily prepared in my past for the present, which were the cause of an excellent preparation for people of the second category, with the help of whom, according to my newly-elaborated plan, the information about the contents of the second series of my books will be given to a larger public, were derived in this way.

When, eight years ago, certain degenerate people, who to the shame of our generation are also called " men ", committed against me an act which became, so to speak, the " apotheosis " of their innumerable " good-deeds ", that is, after my serious motor accident, which was known to all who knew me, and when, thanks to various reasons, obviously deriving, according to law, from the objective good deeds of my ancestors and myself, I, contrary to all expectations, did not die, I soon began to liquidate the Institute founded by me and everything connected with it ; and when, learning later of the hardships of many of the people who had lived for many years at my expense in the main section of the Institute, as well as in other places where I had expected soon to open new sections, I decided to organize for some of them, and their families, a community-life in one of the States of Central Europe, where life was relatively cheap and more or less suitable for such a purpose.

I organized this community-life for those necessitous people, who, while near me, had behaved scrupulously and more or less meritoriously ; and I joined with them those whom I had met on my way from Turkestan to Paris, and whom, as they were not yet ready, I regarded only as candidates to be sent later to the aforesaid monastery in Central Asia.

Since then, all of them are still living there, and, while fulfilling all kinds of inevitable tasks of ordinary life, continue, on the one hand, to carry out in practice the possibilities they had learnt from me during their stay in the Institute, and, on the other, to acquaint themselves thoroughly with all my current work, copies of which are sent to them regularly.

As very many of the people whom I met in the last two decades would be extremely interested to learn what it was that guided me in determining the worthiness of different people for this aim of mine, and, as at the same time, this knowledge, I believe, might become for some of them an immediate incentive factor, making them assimilate at last, although merely for their egotistical benefit, some truth they had learnt from me, I consider it appropriate to state openly here that, from the large amount of data which proved the fitness of these people to me, the principal were the following five :

1) If I established, after-all round observation, that they had had in their individuality, since preparatory age, certain definite starting points for a more or less meritorious life in responsible age.

2) If in their being there were not completely atrophied generally inherited predispositions for the developing in the individuality of factors bringing forth the impulses of " organic-shame ", " religiousness ", " patriarcha-lity ", " the -awareness-of-one's-mortality ", etc.

3) If there was a hereditary predisposition enabling the conscious eradication of previously rooted weaknesses in their individuality, due to abnormal surroudings.

4) If they already gave evidence of having had suitable, established conditions of ordinary life, and had the acquired possibility to attain, according to certain principles, some definite perspectives for the future.

5) If there were present a distinct degree of awareness of their own " nothingness ", and the possibility to attain the necessary quality of desire for transforming themselves from such nothingness into the definite " something ", which they ought to be, even according to their own tranquilly meditated understanding.

Now, subsequent to the above " ground-work ", as the master-painter would say, I have drawn the general outlines of the very essence of my appeal, and I wish to share with you, and to communicate to you, one of the many definite deductions which I made during my long, impartial observations, in the course of special studies of the automatic and sometimes relatively conscious manifestations, of people of the most varying social standing, degrees of innate comprehension, education, race and belief, that is, definite deductions regarding a most pernicious and undesirable factor, and both in the general and in the subjective sense, and one sharply manifested in man's psychic sphere.

For the moment I shall limit myself to mentioning only general information concerning this psychic factor inherent in everyone, which I have verified and elucidated in every possible way, and which amazed me, after appearing to be, at first, relatively insignificant. Later, I shall speak in detail of this factor, as well as of means established by me as a result of my experimental elucidatory methods, which would modify and even destroy completely this undesirable factor with all its consequences.

This psychic factor, amazing to me because of its absolute contradiction to the convictions instilled in me since childhood, as well as to the religious and moral conceptions common to all people today, was observed by me, and later, during the 21 years of artificial life mentioned at the beginning of this booklet, was elucidated in all its aspects, thanks to one of my many principles which I infallibly applied to everybody I met without distinction.

This principle, one of the several I was constantly carrying out during this period, consisted in that I never considered, and under no circumstances encouraged, in the people I met the impulse created by that factor inevitably formed in the general individuality of modern man, the, manifestations of which are known under the names of " Vanity " and " Self-Conceit ", but on the contrary considered myself obliged to adopt a critical attitude towards them, and risked all prosperity depending upon it.

In order to make it clear to all readers and to emphasize its importance, I think it necessary to give the reasons for applying the above-mentioned principle during that period of my life.

Long before that period of my life, when I consciously decided, under special oath, for a definite time to manifest myself and react to the manifestations of the people I met in a certain manner, acting for many years, as I have already noted, as professional hypnotist, although I tried as much as possible, while exercising my profession, to keep under the control of my consciousness the undesirable manifestations of my nature, in spite of this, there gradually formed within me, proceeding far beyond the control of my active consciousness, certain automatic influences upon people around me during their waking as well as their hypnotic state.

On account of this, there soon began to become really perceptible to my awaking consciousness various consequences, irreconcilable with my nature, of this automatic influence over people, which often evoked in me remorse of conscience ; and therefore, in working out the programme of my life, which was to be my guiding principle for the future, and of which the fundamental and chief task was that I always, in the course of this predetermined period, in all the inner states of my organism, ought to '' cultivate '' inwardly and manifest towards everyone I met the feelings of love, pity benevolence, etc., I also decided to include the above-mentioned principle, because its application to life, although mainly to serve my special aim, constituted, in my opinion, at the same time, a part of my inner benevolence towards people.

In this way, creating in my consciousness, which had previously acquired a good stability, not without unceasing struggle with the weaknesses inherent in my nature, I maintained almost always in relation to everyone I met without distinction the aforesaid benevolent impulse ; helping them, for instance, with useful advice, money, and things essential for life, such as food, letters of recommendation, etc. ; as a result, however, of all my observations and enquiries, I most definitely established that all these good deeds of mine did not arouse in them recognition of all my kindness, but, on the contrary, formed in all of them a feeling toward me of evident unfriendliness which was due to the fact that, according to the above-mentioned principle, I did not take into consideration and react to the influence of the " variously-tinted " impulses, which arose in them as a result of the psychic factor common to man today.

In all this, the most curious fact, in my opinion, and one capable of rousing in man a great many reflections, is the one established and verified by me in all its aspects, and which appears to be lawful as well, to the effect that if, in relation to any one of those already harbouring against me such unfriendliness, when I deliberately increased my inner benevolence, increasing proportionally, of course, at the same time the aforesaid " fault-finding ", this unfriendliness increased in all cases without exception and reached a manifest hostility toward me.

While speaking about this pernicious factor existing in every psychic state of the modern man, who has been for so many years one of the principal objects of my special observations, I consider it necessary, before stating my final " conclusion ", to say, first, the following :

In the present period of my life, when declining in years, after having had everything to satiety that life can offer to a human being, and having been thereby fully disillusioned in everything, and consequently possessing in the highest degree all data enabling me to be my impar-

tial, I, calling on Heaven and Earth to witness my since-
rity and swearing by the peace of my conscience after death,
now, based on the convictions established in my consciousness, proclaim in the hearing of all :

The fundamental cause of almost all the misunderstan-
dings arising in the inner world of man, as well as in the
process of the communal life of people, is chiefly this
psychic factor, which is formed in man's being during the
period of preparatory age exclusively on account of a
wrong education, and in the period of responsible age
each stimulation of which gives birth in him to the impulses of „ **Vanity** " and „ **Self-Conceit** ".

I categorically affirm that the happiness and self-
consciousness, which should be in a real man, as well
as in a peaceful communal existence between people
(leaving aside and not attempting to analyse here the
numerous other causes which exist in our lives through no
fault of our own), depend in most cases exclusively on
the absence in us of the feeling of '' Vanity ''.

My most sincere wish in this case is that every man,
who strives to justify before Great Nature his destiny as
a man, and not merely as an animal, that destiny which
is alloted to him among the other Beings on Earth, and is
such as it ought to be (as I prove logically in the third series
of my writings, and affirm without any possible refutation
on anybody's part), should see afterwards, in his endeavour to discover the sense of my writings and in the new
institutions I expect to found, first of all the possibility
of finding in them various means of helping him to eradi-
cate from his entirety those data fixed in him, the totality
of which gives birth to every variety of the feelings of
'' Vanity ''.

And with a view, on the one hand, to characterising
—for the preparation, so to speak, of '' fertile soil ''

enabling readers all the better to grasp my subsequent appeals—my perpetual, as it might be called, " maniacal striving " towards the solution of all as yet obscure " theandrological " problems, and, on the other hand, in order to make my readers understand more clearly the real significance of the presence in men's inner world of factors contributing to a conscious or even an automatic cultivation of good impulses towards other people, from which impulses rise all sorts of consequences contradicting the usual conceptions of men—that is, impulses idealized and professed by all religious doctrines which have existed and still exist on earth, as well as by the morality which the ages have forged in man's life,—I consider it useful or even necessary to confess here that to have the possibility of explaining to myself in more detail the results of the manifestation in human intercourse of a " naked " relationship based on love, pity, trust, sympathy, etc., free from all kinds of evil conventions outwardly established in our life, results that before escaped my attention for some reason, I, from the day I started this my first appeal, up to today, that is, from the 13th of September to the 13th January 1933, on one side began myself to put into practice very insistently, and even with a constant self derision, that religious philosophical principle known by men for centuries, and according to which our ancestors and even some contemporary people who reached, thanks to their good life, a certain degree of self-consciousness, dedicated a third of each year of their life—depending on which part would least interfere with the obligation of their ordinary life,—for self-perfection or, as they say, for " saving their souls " ; this principle could be formulated in this way : ,, **To - be - patient - towards - every - being - and - not - to - attempt - by - the possibilities - in our - power -**

to - alter - the consequences - of - the - evil - deeds - of - our - neighbours ", on the other side, I provoked and supported the manifestations of the principle through an artificial influence on the psyche of three other different persons, and I observed thoroughly all the consequences that resulted from it.

The devices of my artificial influence were threefold :

The first I influenced by means of almost uninterrupted, kindly-intentioned persuasions and conscientious exhortations ; the second I influenced by threats of the terrible future awaiting him, and the third by means of various hypnotic suggestions.

During the same period, in so far as my temporary physical depression, the consequence of serious fatigue, permitted, I still further intensified, in relation to all people coming in contact with me, my inner benevolence, but accompanied it by the strict fulfilment of the possibility set myself as a serious task of always remembering and, in conversations, deliberately manifesting, under a mask of serious irritation, the device I have practised since the beginning of my aforesaid twenty-one year period of artificial life, and which I have summed up in the phrase : **" To-quarrel-ruthlessly-with - all - manifestations - dictated - in - people - by - the - evil - factor - of - vanity - present - in - their-being."**

As to the facts I established at that time, I verified in all their aspects all the new facts which derived from that, so-called " contact of inner worlds ", and I shall speak about them in some subsequent appeals I intend to publish, but I should like, in the meantime,—with reference to the last of my special observations and verifications, which I conducted, of course, also with a view to preparing for our descendants the factual material for the right inculcation and understanding by them of the real and true meaning of the psyche of their " neighbours " and fellow-men, unfortunate creatures, too, on account of their lack of will-power and of real, objective reason, so that they, i. e. our descendants, unlike us who, as people of our times, have already become, by reason of the abnormal environment, almost simple and automatically-vegetating animals, whereas we should be real God-like creatures capable of entering into and understanding the position of others,—to give an approximate explanation in this my first appeal of one original " elucidatory experiment ", attempted by me during the last months, and to confess yet another and new categorical decision, brought forth by the consequences of this very psychological experiment, and to the fulfilment of which decision I intend to proceed immediately upon the completion of all my writings.

I should like to speak of this experiment here and even to confess my categorical decision in this matter, in particular, so that there may arise—in the mentation of the many people who have met me on the ground of my ideas, but who still persist in vegetating on Earth, and on whom I then wasted much time without benefit for either them or myself, chiefly on account of their criminal laziness,— time which did not suffice, as it was, for my very important current affairs on a world scale—some shock of such intensity as to permit the formation in them finally, even if automatically, of some other form of " thinking-and-feeling " more proper to man.

I must state, first of all, that when, during these last months, I was working on this first appeal of mine while simultaneously looking through my first series of writings, which were ready for print, there arose the necessity of elucidating for myself the aforesaid detailed results eluding ordinary observation as to the existence in man's inner world of all sorts of altruistic strivings towards other people, therefore, taking into account the resulting situation, namely, that there were almost no people left about me essential for my general experimental elucidations, which was the consequence of the decision I had been applying over a period of years to limit the circle of people seeking to come in contact with me, I had recourse—in order to have at my disposal once again of the necessary body of various types of people, i. e. to have, as is said, a " wide field for experiment "—to the following measure.

Having decided long beforehand to mortgage, upon the completion of my writings, my two European estates in order that, if upon the completion of my writings, my " collateral-commercial " affairs, as I call them, should happen for some reason, at the moment intended for publication, to be in what is a called a " process-of-increasing-inertia ", which as a matter of fact did happen, I might not be wholly dependent on others, and that I might have the possibility by the help of the money thus realized to put on foot the publication and spreading abroad of my writings as I thought fit, I set about the arranging of this mortgage not as any person more or less familiar with Parisian ways would have done, i. e. by simply entrusting the affair to the nearest lawyer, but, with the intention of forming such on experimental field, entrusted the affair rather to a whole series of special offices existing for this purpose, as well as to private " commission-agents " and " sub-commission-agents ".

Thanks to this, what I think to be my last " extravaganza ", and with a view to satisfying the same mania, I elucidated for my own benefit—besides convincing myself of the correctness of my strange verification, which absolutely contradicted men's usual conception, that the force and degree of man's inner benevolence evokes a proportionate degree of " ill-will " in others,—a multitude of hitherto unsuspected and new, though slight, and yet very significant and explicative facts, and even, it may be said boldly, I became " stuffed " again with such wealth of purely psychological material that, contrary to my conviction, as well as that of all those who have more or less familiarised themselves with my writings, —a conviction that I had nothing more to write about, as Ih ad already written about everything imaginable, it would, perhaps, have sufficed for my new writer's profession for the remainder of my life, assuming of course that I desired to continue in it.

I was enriched to the maximum with material for writing on a countless number of different themes, capable of composing in their totality an important literary work, more extensive even perhaps than " Beelzebub's Tales To His Grandson ", and called this time, for example, " Dreams and Fantasies of People in the Twentieth Century ".

Two other sad consequences must be mentioned with reference to my real situation : the first was that I was forced, during that period, to abandon those places in Paris to which I had become accustomed, and to interrupt often in this way the regular tempo of my thoughts, which were devoted to my given task, because, from the day I had recourse to the aforesaid offices and private persons, the expansion of my " experimental-field " began to assume such proportions, as a result apparently of the general crisis, that within two or three days I was obliged to do so for fear of being, so to speak, finally " sucked dry" ; and the second was in that my extravagant idea cost me in the end a goodly sum of French francs and German marks.

I would not have called this second circumstance sad, as it was all in the order of things to bear heavy expenses in the course of my various psychological researches, had it not been that I unexpectedly became that year a victim of the American crisis as well.

Recalling now this much talked of " American crisis ", and though fully cognizant of the fact that very many will reproach me, I shall not disguise, but openly admit, the fact that not only am I personally content, but that I even experience an impulse of " satisfaction " and bless this crisis, which has shaken what was, to all appearances, an already stable and prosperous American life.

Such an apparently " malignant " impulse arose in my original individuality, and continues to thrive therein, for the present as a result of the fact that only in consequence of its action upon my material position was I afforded the possibility of confirming the correctness of my investigations and have only now come to the full and absolute conviction, expressed now in all my being and not only, as before, in my consciousness, that if, in contradistinction to that documentally verified fact which persisted in the process of the communal life of people up to the famous " Graeco-Roman-Civilisation ", at the present time in the process of our communal life all the inner determined impulses of any man have finally ceased to make any impression and to have of their own accord any reverberation in the inner world of the people around us, this results exclusively from the consequences of the inculcation into the as yet unformed consciousness of the growing generation of various conventions and customs for their artificial manifestation, i. e. as a consequence of their so-called upbringing, which began to assume such distorted forms at the time of the Graeco-Roman civilisation and to flourish particularly in the period of the Middle Ages.

The immediate consequence of this my last " extravaganza " was that, meeting a multitude of people of every kind of social situation and heredity, living at the present time in that centre of communal life for contemporary people which is even termed the " capital of the world ", and where, consequently, must flow all, so to speak, " perfected devices " of happy customary existence and whence all other people ought to take and use these for their good,—among the number of these perfected devices must be counted also, of course, simplified methods for the purposed formation in man's being of corresponding factors for the conscious and automatic manifestation of various aspects of " objective-morality ",—I, having outwardly with these people, on the ground of my wish to obtain a comparatively small sum of money against the security of my property worth many millions, various, so to speak, " logically-sequent-business-relations ", and inwardly realizing in practice the aforesaid " religious-philosophical-principle " in pursuance of my special psychological aim, as a result of all this, have fully and clearly, and without any shadow of doubt, established the complete absence in them of all those psychological factors which, in accordance with many historical data lending themselves to documentary proof, necessarily formed themselves in the entirety of people of past epochs.

Those psychic factors in particular, which form themselves in people during the period of their preparatory age partly of their own accord under the influence of their environment, and partly by the deliberate action of wise tutors, during responsible life, mechanically react in such a way upon the usual general psyche, that these people cannot, even in spite of all their mental desire, behave in relation to others otherwise than in accordance with these psychic factors rooted in them since childhood.

I refer to those factors which are in the process of forming, even in the present time, entirely automatically; it is true, in the majority of people living on all continents in places more or less isolated from the influence of so-called contemporary " culture ".

It must be added here that these psychic factors may likewise be easily instilled into people living their preparatory age under the conditions of contemporary culture, but to make possible the conservation of these factors unchanged over the whole period of responsible life it is indispensable,—with a view to their fixation, as my experimental elucidations have shown me—to watch over them indefatigably over a period of one or two years following their coming of age, and shield them from specially potent environing influences by exercising a corresponding influence over them.

Of these psychic factors the one that stands out most in relief, and which becomes at once easily obvious, is the factor that may be called " scruple-of-conscience " and which makes it impossible that its possesser act otherwise than frankly in relation to all those who show him full inner confidence, even if his so-called " waking-consciousness " urge him to act in an opposite manner.

Speaking of this factor, inherent in the human psyche, which necessarily formed itself and was present in the whole period of the responsible life of our ancestors, now long departed into Eternity, does not prevent my saying also and even emphasizing with an impulse of great offence that of the fifty people inhabiting the capital of the world and serving me at that time—without, of course, their being conscious of it—as objects of my observations and elucidations, the functioning and manifestation of this peculiar psychic factor proved among eleven of them to have been completely transformed into the factor called in ancient times " podispodny ", that is, degeneration, and one which has already gone so far that, on accidental or deliberate excitation of this factor, the manifestation of its action comes about in man by the accomplishment of a diametrically opposite act.

I even assured myself of the existence in two of these eleven persons, two brothers of juridical origin, marked signs of the beginning of that same evil " nothing ", which wa. first noted in man's entirety by the Babylonian sages and physiochemists, and called by them " poisnekuer ", and which, according to the explanation of these sages, has the property of becoming transformed under certain well known conditions of environment into a source of contagion.

I have the intention, I may say, upon the final completion of work on all my writings, to make this " nothing ", also, the object of my investigations and to try and find means for uprooting forever from people's lives this plague on humanity.

And becoming convinced during this time that the principal reason for the absence of these factors, which can be with ease deliberately formed, was to be found chiefly in the absence in the process of our contemporary life, for the education of the growing generation, of those specially trained people, who were necessarily to be found in the process of the customary life of our ancestors and were called " spiritual-instructors ", and whose chief obligation consisted in helping, by direct influence upon the inner world of children in their district, the formation in them of these particular, and inevitably requisite for communal life, psychic factors, I, without long reflection, decided that if I were successful, in the first place,—in successfully overcoming by means of my writings that established and specifically mass psychosis of people, which was already analysed in all its aspects in ancient times and was called " helertoon ", and which may also be explained, according to contemporary understanding, as the " unusual-excitation-of-minds ",—and secondly, in organizing without hindrance, and on the intended " scale-and-tempo ", the clubs of the new type already mentioned, I would introduce from the beginning without fail the idea that one of the principal functions of these clubs should be the rapid organization everywhere among large groups of people of Institutes, the aim of which would be to prepare such " spiritual-instructors " as would fully answer to their calling.

" Aniline-cayenne " will follow from this particular categorical decision of mine because into this decision there enters also my supposition that I, for the possibility of realising my aim, have also the intention of establishing as my first fund such a sum of money as the elucidatory psychological experiment, just explained, has cost me, with the addition of one more nought as interest, and of recovering this sum forcibly by creating lasting moral suffering in those whose duty at one time it was to make manifest the factors of good, giving rise to " scruple of conscience " in the entirety of those people, who lately dealt with with one over the mortgage of my property, —that property earned literally by the sweat of my brow,— which mortgage was necessary for the benefit of humanity ; and I decided to do this with the knowledge and help of their relatives and friends. This will concern, of course, their former and as yet living tutors, for the dead, who did not, while alive, perform their obligations, which they voluntarily undertook towards their successors, annihilate themselves, as I demonstrate experimentally, so completely that, after a few days already, there is no means, either by natural-physical or by supernatural-magical powers, of establishing contact with any of their former parts.

And to make possible the realization of all this, I precisely today and in, to me, a very strange coincidence of circumstances, consisting in that I was writing the last lines of this my first appeal a few minutes before the coming of the New Year, according to the old style, in that moment in particular when, with the passage of objective time, in one of the processes of change from the old to the new year, it suited just and impartial Fate or some other " Saintly-Aspect-of-the-Blessed-Cosmic-Equilibrium " to bring about my appearance into the world, give myself in this, for me, significant moment in the flood of my life, my essential word—to mobilize all my abilities and whatsoever possibilities have accumulated in me in the course of my past life in order to find these people and to realize in relation to them this very aim I have set myself. Amen.

Now, after pronouncing such an often materialised here on Earth, Biblical and all-concluding word, it only remains for me to proclaim to all, who have in any way met me on the ground of my ideas up to the time of my activity as a writer, that, after an eight-year break in all relations with all and sundry, I again eagerly renew them as from today.

I renew them in all eagerness, of course, only with those people whose inner world has not yet finally wasted away and fallen under the sway of various representatives of the God of Evil.

Any personal interview with me is only possible after preliminary correspondence with my secretaries.

Wherever I may be, my permanent address still remains as before : Chateau du Prieuré, Fontainebleau, France.

That place in particular, where was located the chief department of " The Institute For Man's Harmonious Development ", founded by me eleven years ago, and which, I may say, thanks to my keeping in view, from the very beginning of my activity as a writer, that I had in it something indispensable to the aim of fulfilling this present new phase of my activity for the good of my neighbours, and, as a result of this, thanks to the principal aim I had set myself, regardless of my physical state after the catastrophe, of preserving this Chateau, and everything it was comprised of and contained, intact in spite of very considerable difficulties of a material as well as of another nature,—remains at the present time not only intact and as well preserved as it was on the day of my misfortune, but may serve with entire satisfaction—because of the multitude of new constructions and improvements—for all that I may now undertake.

G. Gurdjieff.

CIRCULAR LETTER

addressed to all who have at any time met me on the ground of my ideas, with seven appended registration-blanks.

Dear Sir or Madam,

When looking through, today, the final and printed text of the first book of my writings as it was brought from the printer, and which I have called " The Herald Of Coming Good ", my thoughts began to swarm, like thoroughbred bees disturbed in their narrow, primitive hive, with all sorts of of impressions which had been accumulating in the course of my past life, amongst them the remembrance of definitely elucidated consequences in certain cases whose exterior results were like those which, in my opinion, ought to arise in men's lives through the publication of this book of mine.

While reflecting upon this, as well as upon everything else connected with the ensuing publications of my writings, it occurred to me that, before allowing this which may be called my " Firstborn-on-Earth " to make its initial steps among the masses of people unacquainted with me, I should first send it, armed with my circular letter, to each of those people—granted, of course, I was still able to discover their address—widely scattered over the earth, who have ever come into contact with me on the ground of my ideas and who later deviated from me in the sense of subjective relations towards me as to a personality, no matter whether as friends or enemies.

I decided to do this because this first " child " of mine, forming as it does but a part of a very important general result consequent upon my eight-year, night-and-day, almost uninterrupted, concentrated and unusual, for the contemporay man, active work, lacks still, being as yet isolated, and small into the bargain, sufficient strength to defend itself against all kinds of snares and misfortunes.

The means of defending itself principally against that, of late increased among us, type of people who, though resembling us in outward formation, have yet become in their responsible age as a result of their abnormal education in childhood, as well as, of course, of their degenerate heredity, the possessors of the nature and heredity of real and rapacious ravens.

Sending off this first-born of mine with the prayer of the accompanying letter to shield it from the aforesaid " ravens ", I desire already now, in gratitude for the fulfilment of my request and without waiting for the time to become ripe for this, as it necessarily will, to warn all those who have ever met me, or have discussed my ideas with me, about one condition, as yet unexplained in this booklet, contained in my proposed plan for the spreading far and wide of my writings, which it is my intention also to publish in the near future.

According to this condition for the acquiring of my writings—in spite of what has been said in the text of the booklet herewith appended as to the categorical decision to make accessible only the books of the first series—the books of the second series, as well as the first book of the third series, may also be made as accessible.

The fact is that all the books of the second series will be immediately sent or distributed, as soon as printed, to any one desiring them, irrespective of whether he has already been a follower of mine or has only now become one, to anyone whose address will be indicated on the seven " registration-blanks " appended to this letter, the filling in and posting of which blanks to the corresponding centre for the spreading of my writings being imposed as an obligatory duty upon the person, who will distribute or sell the first three books of the first series of my writings.

I think now it would be most useful—for my fundamental aim as well as for the easy and certain understanding of all I have said in this circular letter of mine— if, in the first place, I frankly confess the objective truth on the basis of which I decided with a clear conscience to make use of such an unusual device for the spreading far and wide of my writings, and, secondly, remind all the honourable addressees of my circular letter of one very actual and and easily imaginable fact, which played a part in my past life during the period of my meetings and discussions with them on the ground of my ideas.

Where the first is concerned, I had in mind that " commandment " already sanctified by the ages for the peaceful and happy existence of communities and which is thus expressed in words : " One-hand-washes-another."

But the last mentioned fact resulted from and consists in that if I—the person, that is, whose common sense, broad understanding, presence of mind and commercial capacities have been briefly but satisfactorily touched upon in the first book of the second series of my writings,—lack,at the present, enough money for the publication, with a view to human happiness, of my almost ten-year's labour as a writer, a labour which is the result of a half-a-century of deliberate suffering and conscious labours for the realization of what was, after all-sided active reflection, predetermined by me, money necessary to avoid depending upon the caprices of various professional and non-professional publishers, then that is due exclusively to the, fact that when I—your formerly " humble servant "— had the opportunity of saving up for such an essential aim this really contemptible money, which is, for contemporary people, the source of most evils, I gave all my time up to you. And you thanks only to this, if you do not possess, chiefly because of your criminal laziness, and also because, I confess now, meeting you then as I did, I was inwardly pursuing an altogether different aim, that which you ought to have, and which, when I then satisfied, with complete honesty on my side, your curiosity, and sometimes even perhaps your love of knowledge, you acquired imperceptibly from yourself and have now in your individuality : first of all, the necessary feeling of " self-valuation ", which gives you the possibility of feeling yourself superior to the average man, and, secondly, you have in you the preliminary required data for entering with the help of my detailed and written explanations and indications upon the path leading to real Being.

I think I have the right to ask from you still more, namely, that you, as people more or less familiar with my language and the form taken by my thought, as well as with my original manner of exposition, should first attempt yourselves, without any of that " philosophising " common to contemporary people, to understand the various axioms illuminated by me in these first books and which in their inter-relation form the very essence of the whole of this series of my impartial writings, and should then devote the whole of yourself, for a definite period, to aiding by your explanations the understanding of them by other of the sons of Our Common Father, who have strayed like you and who lack as a result, as you in your inner world, all perseverance in regard to objective truths of whatsoever nature.

As I was obliged to address this first circular letter principally to people who have already come into direct relation to me, I should like to profit by this opportunity and to express in conclusion in the name of future generations as well as personally my sincere gratitude to those of the people coming into contact with me during the twenty-year-period of life mentioned in the " Herald-Of-Coming-Good ", who have through many years—without their knowledge—served me as objects of my observations and investigations of the processes going on in them of crystallisation and decrystallisation of those psychic factors, the transformation of which for the acquiring of subjectivised manifestation demands a comparatively lengthy period.

I consider it my moral duty to add here that these observations and investigations of mine in the past cannot henceforth serve as the reason why these people, who have served as the objects of my investigation, should now have lost the possibility of entering together with others upon the true path and of attaining—by the help of my detailed and written explanations—to real Being.

For the automatic elimination from the general entity of the above-mentioned people of all psychic factors, capable of impeding the whole hearted devotion of self to newly based work for the attainment of the predetermined Higher Being, which must necessarily be kin to man, and for the elimination likewise of some resulting and so-called " bitter-dregs " in relation to me as a personality, I think it is necessary to say only the following :—

Believe me, during the whole period of my relations with you, my inner world never harboured either egotistical or altruistic impulses, and there existed only, always and in everything, the exclusive desire to prepare in all perfection for the future generations the science of the " Objective-Truth-Of-Reality ".

But know, in any case, that, firstly, the whole amount realized by the sale of the books of my first series of writings, will be carried into a special fund, reserved for printing, the spreading of these writings among the masses and the giving of facilities to those unable to acquire them, and, secondly, all detailed enquiries as to the all—embracing literature created by me during these years will be answered for the time being only from the central bureau of my publications whose address is : Chateau " Paradou ", Fontainebleau, France.

At the moment the first book of the first series is already being set up and printed in the Russian, French, English and German colloquial languages ; translations are already being finished in the Armenian, Spanish, Turkish and Swedish languages.

So far the books of the first series are being printed only in France ; in the near future it is proposed to begin printing in Germany, America and Persia.

For the retail sale of the first edition of the books of this first series I fix the price—irrespective of the place of sale— at 200 French francs.

G. GURDJIEFF.

A SUPPLEMENTARY ANNOUNCEMENT

Evoked by the Events of the Last few days and Which Might Have Very Great Significance For Many People Who Have Known Me.

Tuesday, 7th March 1933.
Grand Café.
Fontainebleau.

The events of an economic, political and social character, taking place in the past few weeks among the people of all the continents, have finally confirmed in me the conviction that already this small booklet of my writings, which heads the list of my publications, will have an unusually large and moreover a rapidly increased circulation and will fall, of course, first of all into the hands of each one of those people who, eleven years ago, took part in one way or another in the organization in France of the principal department of the public institute founded by me under the name of " The Institute For Man's Harmonious Development ".

And in view of the fact that, shortly on that very spot, and in almost the same conditions, there is due to take place a very important event connected with that former organization, I decided today, that is, a few hours before the appearance of this book in print, when I was sketching the plans of my proposed new constructions, to write the following announcement and to ask the publisher to add this supplement.

This imminent event, information about which will without doubt call up in the feelings and thought of all those who formerly participated in my past activity various associations and reactions, consists in that, firstly, -on the 23rd of April by the old style of the real year, that is, on the day of Saint-George-the-

Victor, which day was counted throughout the period of the existence of the Institute as, so to speak, its " Coronation-Day ", there is due to take place, as also happened for the first time eleven years ago, a solemn laying of the foundation stone of the new building, which already, in its first form, was, on account of its significance, considered and ought henceforth all the more to be considered as it were as the heart of all my activity for the good of my neighbours and which was known to all who ever visited the Chateau du Prieuré under the name of " Gymnasium " or, as it was called by the English and Americans, " Study-House ".

This time, the final building, answering as it does in every respect to its appelation will be situated in the very centre of the big park.

The new " Gymnasium " or " Study-House " will comprise, besides the theatre and lecture hall which already existed, on the first and basement floors several independent laboratories, fitted out according to all the achievements of modern science, and in the number of which will be found three as yet unexistent on Earth, namely the " Magnetic-Astral ", the " Thoughthanbled-zoin " and Mentaloethero-winged ; above will be the also fabulous, astronomical observatory fitted out with all devices for applying all the laws known on Earth in various ages for the refraction and reflection of rays and for the magnifying of the visibility by means of mediumistic properties.

This building will be fitted out also with other inventions, which I long ago constructed and which are already known to many, though they have not been as yet exploited, and among which are to be found : The " Luminous-Key-Board " and the " Retro-Rebounding-Echoraising-Organ ".

Secondly, from the first of June of this year will be established again the interrupted activity of the Institute organized at that time, though it is being re-established on other foundations and even under an altogether different name, but appearing in its totality as the result of its realization at that time.

There will be re-established also in its full intensity that activity which is so unusual in modern times and which was first interrupted in 1924 as a result of the serious injuries which I received in my motor accident, and also later as a result of my decision to devote myself wholly for a definite period to activity as a writer.

I have now decided, in this first booklet to be published by me and which might also be called, as they used to say in ancient times, " Habarchi ", i. e. " town-crier ", because it proclaims, above all, in the hearing of all the coming on God's Earth in sequent order of the already weighty, and all-and everything-illuminating volumes written by me, to announce this also in order that—in time for such an impending event which is so significant for the fundamental aim of my life—information about it might have time to reach as great a number of people as possible who participated the first time in the arrangement and opening of the initial activity of the Institute founded by me and to call up in them :—in some, whose actions were at that time based upon a desire for good and happiness not only for themselves, but also for their neighbours, a proud-and-joyful satisfaction ; in others, whose every intention and manifestation was founded upon, as they, too, will now themselves in all probability confess with an impulse of remorse, only their purely-slavish egotism and criminal laziness,— shame and repentance.

And may this my new beginning be in harmony with all the three embodied Blessed Forces of OUR COMMON FATHER. Amen.

ACHIEVED PRINTED ON THE TWENTY
SIXTH OF AUGUST NINETEEN
HUNDREDS AND THIRTY THREE BY
LA SOCIETE ANONYME DES EDITIONS
DE L'OUEST, 40, RUE DU CORNET,
ANGERS (FRANCE).

REGISTRATION BLANK

A N⁰ 00979

for a preliminary subscription to the books of the first series

of writings by **G. GURDJIEFF**

Detachable Subscription-Blank No 7. Sheet A.   N⁰ 00979

1. Name and address of subscriber............................
2. Name and address of person by whom recommended. ....
3. Name and address of the person who first began
   to spread and explain the ideas and writings of
   G. Gurdjieff in the given district.........................
4. Language preferred for reading...........................
5. Did subscriber formerly belong to any group
   associated with M. Gurdjieff's ideas? Where
   and when? ....
   ....

Detachable Subscription-Blank No 6. Sheet A.   N⁰ 00979

1. Name and address of subscriber............................
2. Name and address of person by whom recommended. ....
3. Name and address of the person who first began
   to spread and explain the ideas and writings of
   G. Gurdjieff in the given district.........................
4. Language preferred for reading...........................
5. Did subscriber formerly belong to any group
   associated with M. Gurdjieff's ideas? Where
   and when?...
   ....

Detachable Subscription-Blank No 5. Sheet A.   N⁰ 00979

1. Name and address of subscriber............................
2. Name and address of person by whom recommended. ....
3. Name and address of the person who first began
   to spread and explain the ideas and writings of
   G. Gurdjieff in the given district.........................
4. Language preferred for reading...........................
5. Did subscriber formerly belong to any group
   associated with M. Gurdjieff's ideas? Where
   and when?...
   ....

Detachable Subscription-Blank No 4. Sheet A. N⍛ 00979

1. Name and address of subscriber...........................
2. Name and address of person by whom recommended. ....
3. Name and address of the person who first began to spread and explain the ideas and writings of G. Gurdjieff in the given district.........................
4. Language preferred for reading ....
5. Did subscriber formerly belong to any group associated with M. Gurdjieff's ideas? Where and when?...
....

Detachable Subscription-Blank No 3. Sheet A. N⍛ 00979

1. Name and address of subscriber...........................
2. Name and address of person by whom recommended. ....
3. Name and address of the person who first began to spread and explain the ideas and writings of G. Gurdjieff in the given district.........................
4. Language preferred for reading.............................
5. Did subscriber formerly belong to any group associated with M. Gurdjieff's ideas? Where and when?...
....

Detachable Subscription-Blank No 2. Sheet A. N⍛ 00979

1. Name and address of subscriber...........................
2. Name and address of person by whom recommended. ....
3. Name and address of the person who first began to spread and explain the ideas and writings of G. Gurdjieff in the given district.........................
4. Language preferred for reading ....
5. Did subscriber formerly belong to any group associated with M. Gurdjieff's ideas? Where and when?...
....

Detachable Subscription-Blank No 1. Sheet A. N⍛ 00979

1. Name and address of subscriber...........................
2. Name and address of person by whom recommended. ....
3. Name and address of the person who first began to spread and explain the ideas and writings of G. Gurdjieff in the given district.........................
4. Language preferred for reading ....
5. Did subscriber formerly belong to any group associated with M. Gurdjieff's ideas? Where and when? ....
....

Antonie, Dr. **AURUM POTABILE, OR THE RECEIPT OF DOCTOR FATHER ANTONIE,** Showing His Way and Method. How He Made and Prepared That Most Excellent Medicine for the Body of Man. #95-8. $1.95

Artephius. **THE SECRET BOOK OF ARTEPHIUS,** Written in the Twelfth Century. "Antimony is a mineral participating of Saturnine parts..." #28-1. $2.95

Bacon, Roger. **THE ROOT OF THE WORLD.** The operation of the elements in forty-seven revealing steps. #42-7. $2.95

Bangs, Merwin & Co. **CATALOGUE OF BOOKS ON HERMETIC PHILOSOPHY;** Being the Entire Collection of General E.A. Hitchcock. Hitchcock's own annotations are interspersed. #33-8. $3.95

Boehme, Jacob. **A DISCOURSE BETWEEN A SOUL HUNGRY AND THIRSTY ... AND A SOUL ENLIGHTENED.** The way from darkness to true illumination. #89-3. $3.95

Boehme, Jacob. **OF THE SUPERSENSUAL LIFE,** Or The Life That Is Above Sense, In a Dialogue Between a Disciple and his Master. #90-7. $4.95

Budge, E.A. Wallis. **ANCIENT EGYPTIAN THEOLOGY.** Well illustrated work on Egyptian theological systems and dogmas. #91-5. $5.95

Budge, E.A. Wallis. **THE BANDLET OF RIGHTEOUSNESS:** An Ethiopian Book of the Dead. The spells and rituals of this curious Christian text includes language usually associated with more ancient funerary rites. Translated from the Coptic. #23-0. $3.95

Collin, Rodney. **THE CHRISTIAN MYSTERY.** Contains a provocative section entitled "Litany for the Enneagram" & Collin's interpretation of esoteric Christianity. #26-5. $3.95

Collin, Rodney. **THE HERALD OF HARMONY.** A paean to Gurdjieff and Ouspensky, and their mission as harbingers of the New Age. A rare and valuable document for Gurdjieffian studies. #27-3. $3.95

Cremer, John. **THE TESTAMENT OF CREMER, THE ENGLISHMAN,** Abbot of Westminster, and Friar of the Benedictine Order. Cremer received the secrets of the great Work from the Blessed Raymond. #96-6. $1.95

Darmesteter, James. (tr.) **THE ZEND AVESTA OF ZARATHUSTRA.** Many excellent selections from the enigmatical Zend. #41-9. $5.95

Dee, John. **THE HIEROGLYPHIC MONAD.** The symbolic mathematics of existence in twenty four theorems. Numerous line drawings accompany the text. #54-0. $7.95

Delphinas. **THE BOOK OF LAMBSPRING, A NOBLE ANCIENT PHILOSOPHER, CONCERNING THE PHILOSPHICAL STONE.** Marvelously illustrated with fifteen plates. #92-3. $5.95

Ellam, J.E. **BUDDHISM AND LAMAISM: A STUDY OF THE RELIGION OF TIBET.** Cogent look at Tibetan Buddhist doctrine, custom, and literature. #79-6. $6.95

Faraday, Winifred. **THE DRUIDIC TRIADS,** or The Wisdom of the Cymry. The ethical remnants of a 'lost' oral tradition. #85-0. $5.95

Freher, Dionysius. **OF THE ANALOGY IN THE PROCESS OF THE PHILOSOPHIC WORK, TO THE REDEMPTION OF MAN, THROUGH JESUS CHRIST, ACCORDING TO THE WRITINGS OF JACOB BOEHME.** #10-9. $2.95

Geber, the Arabian. **OF FURNACES.** The ways of their Operation, illustrated, with a glossary appended. #38-9. $5.95

Geber, the Arabian. **OF THE INVESTIGATION, OR SEARCH OF PERFECTION.** Translated by Richard Russell in 1678. #08-7. $2.95

H.T.S. **THE SYSTEM OF PLOTINUS:** A Synthesis of Plotinian Philosophic Religious Mysticism. A fine introduction to Neoplatonism. Charts showing the relationship of various Plotinian principles invaluable. #75-3. $6.95

Hartmann, Franz. **ALCHEMY.** Hartmann's forty three AXIOMATA HERMETICA are included. #24-9. $2.95

Hartmann, Franz. **ROSICRUCIAN SYMBOLS**. The rules, duties, and secret signs of the Rosicrucians. Also, "Signs from the Heart of the Celestial Mother" from AUGUST VINDELICORUM of Antonio Gintner, 1741 is included. #15-X. $2.95

Helvetius. **THE GOLDEN CALF**, Which the World Worships and Adores: In Which is Discussed The Most Rare Miracle of Nature in the Transmutation of Metals. #43-5. $3.95

Janus Lacinius Therapus. **A FORM AND METHOD OF PERFECTING BASE METALS**. A tale of SOLVE ET COAGULA, the death of kings, and the resurrection of the Kingly. This valuable text is heavily illustrated. #04-4. $3.95

Lover of Philalethes. **A SHORT INQUIRY INTO THE HERMETIC ART**. London, 1714. Edited by W.W. Westcott for his Collectanea Hermetica series. #06-0. $4.95

Lully, Raymond. **THE HERMETIC MERCURIES OF RAYMOND LULLY**. With a preface and notes by J.S. Weidenfeld. #36-2. $3.95

Maier, Michael. **A SUBTLE ALLEGORY CONCERNING THE SECRETS OF ALCHEMY**, Being Very Useful To Possess and Pleasant to Read. One of the few in English by the author of ATALANTA FUGIENS. #17-6. $3.95

Massey, Gerald. **GNOSTIC AND HISTORIC CHRISTIANITY**. The supreme gnosis derived from Egypt and the Essenes. #51-6. $5.95

Mead, G.R.S. **THE ORPHIC PANTHEON**. The procession of the Divine and natural powers as recognized in the Orphic Mysteries. #18-4. $6.95

Mead, G.R.S. **PLOTINUS**. Mead's contribution to Neo-Platonic studies with a short bibliography appended. #01-X. $5.95

Nicholson, Reynold. **THE ESSENCE OF SUFISM**. The religious philosophy of Islam as presented by the Sufis. #49-4. $2.95

Nicholson, Reynold. **THE SUFI DOCTRINE OF THE PERFECT MAN**. The Perfect Man as Cosmic Principle, half-Divine, half-human. #48-6. $3.95

Paracelsus. **THE AURORA OF THE PHILOSOPHERS**. Concerns the ancient Magi, the Secret Fire, and the origin of the Philosopher's Stone. #50-8. $3.95

Paracelsus. **THE BOOK OF THE REVELATION OF HERMES**, Interpreted by Theophrastus Paracelsus, Concerning the Supreme Secret of the World. #81-8. $2.95

Paracelsus. **COELUM PHILOSOPHORUM, OR THE BOOK OF VEXATION**. The Science and Nature of Alchemy and What Opinion Should Be Formed Thereof. #13-3. $2.95

Paracelsus. **CONCERNING THE SPIRITS OF THE PLANETS**. A selection of three treatises relating to the elementaries of the planets and the medium of tinctures. #41-1. $2.95

Paracelsus. **HERMETIC ASTRONOMY**. This work contains "The Interpretation and Consideration of the Stars" & "The End of Birth." #09-5. $4.95

Paracelsus. **PARACELSUS' ALCHEMICAL CATECHISM**. This piece was said to have been found in the Vatican Library by the Swiss Mason, Baron Tschoudy. Some rare illustrations included. #03-6. $3.95

Paracelsus. **THE TINCTURE OF THE PHILOSOPHERS**. By the art of Vulcan (the separation of good from evil), three essences pass into one. #45-1. $2.95

Philalethes, Eirenius. **AN OPEN ENTRANCE TO THE CLOSED PALACE OF THE KING**. The medicinal, chemical, and physical arcana in thirty five chapters. #21-4. $4.95

Philalethes, Eirenius. **PREPARATIONS OF THE SOPHIC MERCURY**. This piece last appeared in COLLECTANEA CHEMICA. #05-2. $1.95

Philalethes, Eirenius. **THE SECRET OF THE IMMORTAL LIQUOR CALLED ALKAHEST**. As revealed in forty-three questions and answers. #40-0. $2.95

Plotinus. **ARE THE STARS CAUSES?** Plotinus questions planetary effects in the moral and physical life of Man. #93-1. $2.95

Porphyry. **THE LIFE OF PLOTINUS.** Porphyry was Plotinus' editor as well as his biographer. He arranged the Enneads into the form we now know them, being pleased with the combination of the perfect six with the nines. #12-5. $3.95

Ripley, George. **THE BOSOM BOOK OF GEORGE RIPLEY,** Canon of Bridlington, Containing His Philosophical Accurtations in Making the Philosopher's Mercury and Elixirs. #31-1. $3.95

Scotus, Michael. **CURIOUS INVESTIGATION CONCERNING THE NATURE OF THE SUN AND MOON.** #94-X. $2.95

Shipton, Mother. **THE PROPHESIE OF MOTHER SHIPTON & THE STRANGE AND WONDERFULL PROPHESIES OF LADY AUDELEY.** A reprint of two English catch-pennys of 1641 and 1649. #22-2. $2.95

Smith the Platonist, John. **THE EXCELLENCY AND NOBLENESS OF THE TRUE RELIGION.** The germ of the great Cambridge Platonist' essay on Religion's Rise and Original to it's Term and End. #35-4. $4.95

South, Thomas. **THE ENIGMA OF ALCHEMY.** This fragment of the famous 'lost' poem by the father of Mary Anne Atwood was discovered in a London bookshop. #19-2. $2.95

Starkey, George. **THE OIL OF SULPHUR,** or the Admirable Efficacy and Almost Incredible Virtue of True Oil Which is Made of the Sulphur Vive Set on Fire and Commonly Called Oil of Sulphur Per Campanam. #20-6. $2.95

Taylor, Thomas. (tr.) **APULEIUS ON THE GOD OF SOCRATES.** From the Latin, this translation appeared in 1822. Gods and daemons in the ancient world. #25-7. $4.95

Taylor, Thomas (tr.) **THE LIFE OF PROCLUS BY MARINUS.** From the 1788 edition, this biography of the famed Neoplatonist also exhibits his Nativity figure. #57-5. $5.95

Taylor, Thomas. (tr.) **PLOTINUS' ESSAY ON THE BEAUTIFUL.** Contains the original introduction and notes done by Taylor to accompany the translation. #86-9. $6.95

Taylor, Thomas. (tr.) **PYTHAGOREAN PRECEPTS.** The teachings of Pythagoras as handed down by his followers. The Sentences of Stobaeus are also contained herein. #00-1. $6.95

Unknown German Sage. **A VERY BRIEF TRACT CONCERNING THE PHILOSOPHICAL STONE.** this work is often referred to as **THE BOOK OF ALZE.** #99-0. $2.95

Urbigerus, Baro. **THE ONE HUNDRED ALCHEMICAL APHORISMS.** Brief, concise way to the Work. **THE SUMMARY OF PHILOSOPHY** by Nicholas Flamel is appended. #55-9. $3.95

Vaughan, Thomas. (Eugenius Philalethes). **ANTHROSPOSOPHIA THEOMAGICA.** Provocative analysis of the four elements and the Mystery of Man. #76-1. $4.95

Vaughan, Thomas. **AULA LUCIS,** or The House of Light. "There is a white magic this book is enchanted withal: it is an adventure for Knights of the Sun..." #29-X. $3.95

Vaughan, Thomas. **THE FRATERNITY OF THE ROSY CROSS AND SHORT DECLARATION OF THEIR PHYSICAL WORK.** Written in 1652, the notes are by Waite. Illustrated. #07-9. $5.95

Vaughan, Thomas. **A NOTEBOOK.** More personal than alchemical, this document does speak of his greatest triumph in the Work, the loss of the secret, and its recovery through the grace of God. #11-7. $1.95

Westcott, William Wynn. (ed.) **THE CHALDEAN ORACLES ATTRIBUTED TO ZOROASTER,** Valuable source for Neo-Platonic studies. #16-8. $5.95

Westcott, William Wynn. **ROSICRUCIAN THOUGHTS ON THE EVER-BURNING LAMPS OF THE ANCIENTS.** A very early Westcott piece! Reviews the legends and realities of perpetual Light through the ages. #56-7. $2.95

Westcott, William Wynn. **THE SCIENCE OF ALCHYMY.** First published in 1895, this historical essay reflects many Order of the Golden Dawn ideas relating to Alchemy and its place in the Mystery Tradition. #02-8. $2.95

FOR A COMPLETE LIST OF PUBLICATIONS,
PLEASE ADDRESS:
HOLMES PUBLISHING GROUP
P.O. BOX 623
EDMONDS, WA 98020